BOMBER
SQUADRONS
AT WAR

*Dedicated to all 'Heinz Varieties', past and present,
and to all who served with 'Six-thirty'.*

BOMBER SQUADRONS AT WAR

Nos 57 and 630 Squadrons

GEOFF D. COPEMAN

FOREWORD BY AIR MARSHAL
SIR IVOR BROOM

SUTTON PUBLISHING

First published in the United Kingdom in 1997 by
Sutton Publishing Limited · Phoenix Mill
Thrupp · Stroud · Gloucestershire · GL5 2BU

British Library Cataloguing in Publication Data
A catalogue record for this book is available from the British Library.

ISBN 0-7509-1710-5

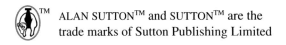 ALAN SUTTON™ and SUTTON™ are the
trade marks of Sutton Publishing Limited

Typeset in 10/12pt Times.
Typesetting and origination by
Sutton Publishing Limited.
Printed in Great Britain by
WBC Limited, Bridgend.

Contents

Foreword

Air Marshal Sir Ivor Broom KCB, CBE, DSO, DFC**, AFC

My mind boggles at the extensive research which has taken place to produce this fascinating and very detailed history of Nos 57 and 630 Squadrons.

No. 57 Squadron's illustrious history stretches from the present back to the days of the Royal Flying Corps and highlights the minuscule flying experience of those aviation pioneers in the First World War. The book describes, in a very objective and undramatic way, the month-by-month successes and sacrifices of No. 57 Squadron members throughout the squadron's long existence. On the other hand, No. 630 Squadron, which was formed at East Kirkby initially from B Flight of No. 57 Squadron, only existed for 20 months in the Second World War, but it experienced continuous action alongside its founding squadron – thus earning a place in RAF history.

The author never forgets the contribution which the ground crew make – and always make – to the success of any squadron. Long hours in the open air on new airfields with primitive living and working conditions in some of the severe winter weather which often prevailed during the Second World War never deterred them. Seven days a week, working long hours each day, was common for them during the war, and they will always be remembered with pride.

Ivor Broom

Acknowledgements

I extend my grateful thanks to all who have helped in the preparation of this work, including the staff of the Imperial War Museum, London; the Public Record Office, Kew; the Library of the Royal Air Force Museum, Hendon; MOD S10 (Air), RAF Innsworth, Gloucester; the Air Historical Branch, MOD. Thanks are also due to the many ex-members and friends from 57 and 630 Squadrons: Frank Beasley, Gerry Beauvoisin, Eric Blanchard, Denis Brown, John Chatterton, Christopher Chester-Jones, Malcolm Crapper, Sidney Culver, Denis Edgley, Jonathan Falconer, Les Gillard, Peter Grimwood, Roland Hammersley, Keith Handscomb, John Holmes, Denis Howell, Allen Hudson, Angus Irwin, Bob Jefcoate, John Johnson, Roy Jones, Rory O'Brien, John MacBean, Len Manning, Peter R. March, Mary Marsden, Jerry Monk, Jan Mulder, Auke Noordhof, Fred and Harold Panton, Ted Querzani, Kay Rowland, Fraser Smith, Eric Snell, Sidney Tidey, Vic Tomei, Alan Turner, Tom Vaisey, Les Wakerell, Bill Waterhouse, Stan White. Finally, to my wife, Elizabeth, for her unending patience.

    I extend apologies to those left off the list.

THE LINCOLNSHIRE AVIATION HERITAGE CENTRE

The photographs on pp. 115 and 133 show details of the memorial plaques. This memorial, unveiled in October 1979, to the memory of the members of Nos 57 and 630 Squadrons lost in action, stands on the site where stood the guardroom of RAF East Kirkby, and also marks the entrance to the Lincolnshire Aviation Heritage Centre.

    Determined that memories of the East Kirkby airfield's past shall not be lost, farmers Fred and Harold Panton established the centre on a part of the site. It is dedicated to the memory of Bomber Command and, in particular, to their brother, Christopher, killed on the Nuremburg raid.

    The Flying Control Tower has been restored to its 1944 appearance and a hangar, built on the base where No. 2 Hangar stood, houses Lancaster NX611, now named *City of Sheffield* and coded 'DX-C' on the starboard side and 'LE-C' on the port. The unique collection, on the A155 between Coningsby and Spilsby, is open every day except Sundays.

GLOSSARY OF TERMS AND ABBREVIATIONS

AA/ack-ack	Anti-aircraft fire (British)
AC1, 2	Aircraftman 1st, 2nd Class
AFC	Air Force Cross
AG	Air gunner
AM	Air Mechanic
AOC-in-C	Air Officer Commanding-in-Chief
'Archie'	RFC's nickname for enemy anti-aircraft fire. (Music-hall song of the time: 'Archibald, certainly not!')
ARP	Air Raid Precautions
Bandit/intruder	Enemy aircraft on airfield circuit
BEF	British Expeditionary Force
BEM	British Empire Medal
Bods	Airmen
CO	Commanding Officer
Comm. Site	Communal (living) Site
Con. Unit or HCU	Heavy Conversion Unit
'Cookie'	Nickname for a 4,000 lb High Capacity (blast) Bomb
DFC	Distinguished Flying Cross
DFM	Distinguished Flying Medal
DI	Daily Inspection
Double BST	British Summer Time became the norm for winter in the Second World War. Clocks were moved forward for a further hour in the spring
Dreidekker	Fokker triplane
DSO	Distinguished Service Order
Eindekker	Fokker monoplane
Erks/Irks	Airmen of lowly rank
ETA	Estimated Time of Arrival
Fee	Nickname for a FE2b aircraft
'Fishpond'	An airborne radar
Flak	Enemy anti-aircraft fire (from *Flugabwehrkanone*)
'Gardening'	Code-name for mine-laying operations
GD	General Duties
'Gee'	A radio navigational aid
GM	George Medal
GP	General Purpose (bombs)
HDU	Hose Delivery Unit
HE	High explosive
HLB	High Level Bombing
'Hostile', HA	Enemy aircraft
HQ	Headquarters
H2S	An airborne radar navigational aid
i/c	In charge
Intercom	Intercommunication (aircraft)
'Jabs'	Inoculations
KD	Khaki Drill uniform

LAC/LACW	Leading Aircraftman/woman
MALM	Master Air Loadmaster
MBE	Member of the British Empire Order
MO	Medical Officer
MT	Motor Transport
M/UG	Mid-upper gunner
NAAFI (Naffy)	Navy, Army & Air Forces Institutes
NCO	Non-commissioned Officer
NFT	Night Flying Test
OC	Officer Commanding
Ops, sorties	Operations
ORB	Operations Record Book (Form 540)
ORs	Other ranks
OTU	Operational Training Unit
PFF	Pathfinder Force
Pusher	Aircraft with the propeller behind the engine
QRA	Quick Reaction Alert
Quirk	Nickname for BE2c aircraft
RAAF	Royal Australian Air Force
RAE	Royal Aircraft Establishment
RCAF	Royal Canadian Air Force
Rigger	Traditional term for Airframe Fitter
RNZAF	Royal New Zealand Air Force
R/T	Radio telephone
R/V	Rendezvous point
S.	Serviceable
SAAF	South African Air Force
Schrägemusik (lit. 'wild music')	German code-name for fighter aircraft fitted with upward-firing guns
SHQ	Station Headquarters
SP	Service policeman
Tail-dragger	Aircraft with a tail-skid or tail wheel
TI	Target Indicator
Tractor	Aircraft with the propeller in front of the engine
Tripehounds, Trips	Sopwith Triplanes
U/S	Unserviceable
USAAF	United States Army Air Force
USAF	United States Air Force (post-WWII)
u/t	Under training
Vegetable	Code-name for airborne sea-mine
V1 ('Doodle-bug')	German flying bomb
V2	German rocket weapon
WAAF	Women's Auxiliary Air Force
Waaf	A member of the WAAF
'Window'	Code-name for metallized paper strips dropped from Allied bomber aircraft and used to foil enemy radar (now known as 'chaff')
W/Op	Wireless Operator

CHAPTER I

Formation and the First 'Blooding'

Almost from the inception of the Royal Flying Corps it became common practice for squadrons to train their own pilots and, eventually, other aircrew, from scratch so that almost every aerodrome served as an Initial Flying School. Thus, as the First World War ground on, and more and more volunteers came forward to learn the arts of aviation, it was to the earliest squadrons that the task of creating new units fell. By 1916, with the primary task of defending the north of England against the Zeppelin night-raiders, No. 33 (Home Defence) Squadron, stationed at Bramham Moor, Yorkshire, was well fitted for these training duties.

By the early summer of 1916, as the Allies prepared for 'The Big Push' that would launch the five-month Battle of the Somme, a surplus of embryo pilots was beginning to build up at Bramham and the foundation of a new squadron was put in hand. When Air Mechanic Bill Waterhouse was told, on returning from weekend furlough, that he had been posted to No. 57 Squadron he was surprised to find that for a few days he was the new unit's sole member. However, the ex-infantryman, just eighteen years old, was soon joined by others and by 2 June the squadron had become a distinct unit under the command of Second Lieutenant A.M. Lavery.

Their transport consisted of a 3-ton lorry, a Crossley tender and a Phelan & Moore motor-cycle as they set off for Copmanthorpe, 10 miles away, where they erected two portable hangars and half-a-dozen bell-tents. The squadron was formally established on 8 June and on 14 June Captain (later Major) L.A. Pattinson MC arrived to assume command.

A mixed bag of twelve aircraft, mostly BE2cs and a few Avros made up the initial equipment. The BEs, known – without great affection – as 'Quirks', were hand-me-downs from No. 33 Squadron and were in various states of serviceability, while the Gnome Monosoupape engines of the Avros proved so unreliable that these were used only for dual training.

Until sufficient qualified pilots joined 57's nominal roll, trainees received instruction from 33's CO, Major Joubert,[1] Flt Sgt T. Warren and 1st AM Shaw. Shaw was an accomplished pilot but, so the story goes, rather blotted his copybook. Apparently, he took great delight in making the wheels of his BE spin by touching them on the backs of grazing cattle; a slight misjudgement resulted in a wrecked Quirk, a dead cow and an immediate posting.

Where elementary flying takes place life is never dull and there was another memorable occasion during the short stay at Copmanthorpe when an Armstrong Whitworth FK8 landed short of petrol and was refuelled with water. Later on, the reverse happened; petrol got into the water-jacket and the engine blew up.

As the squadron grew, responsibility for training the newly arrived officers fell upon the few experienced pilots on the unit's strength. One of those to join in this capacity was Nicholas Comper who left the Service many years later to form the company that produced the famous though diminutive Comper Swift monoplane. Among the earliest pupils was Donald Healey who achieved success with his sports cars in later life. Flying went on from dawn to dusk as weather permitted and, in time, better machines became available, though only in the form of later marks of the Quirk.

Bill Waterhouse in the cockpit of a BE2c (W. Waterhouse)

In August the unit returned to Bramham Moor. The troops were now unable to make the short walk into York for entertainment but were obliged to look elsewhere. Leeds was the obvious magnet for most, but a long way off. On alternate Saturdays the squadron transport ran into the city, ostensibly to the public baths. These trips were eagerly awaited, though not necessarily for purposes of either cleanliness or Godliness.

It was a strict rule that each squadron should await its fortnightly turn but the rule was flouted shamelessly. On one occasion, their vehicle having broken down, No. 33 Squadron borrowed 57's lorry. When the vehicle began the return journey, the driver complained to the senior officer of overloading. The officer, one of 33's more officious Sergeant-Majors, ordered a roll-call and, on discovering that the lorry had been burdened with eighty-seven passengers, decreed that 57's share should walk the remaining twelve miles to camp. He was determined to make his decision stand, ignoring appeals made on behalf of a crippled airman, lately of the cavalry, who thus had to be carried by his comrades. The following morning the Warrant Officer concerned learned that Major Pattinson shared the opinions of his men about this heartless attitude.

By 25 October the full complement of operational aircraft, eighteen FE2cs, had arrived and the squadron was ready for working up into a fighting unit. The role assigned was that of 'Army Fighters', a curious description, as at no time did their operational orders seem to expect them to work as 'fighters' as the term is understood today.

Even by the standards of the day the FE2 was an odd affair with its 'pusher' propeller at the back and a curious cockpit at the front for the observer/gunner. However, it was highly thought of by those whose job it was to buy aircraft, less so by those who flew them. With a 50-feet wingspan it was nearly half as big again as many of its contemporaries. It was almost impossible to make it dive and so stable was the design that, as speed built up, the 'Fee' would simply level out.

The version flown by 57 was powered by a 250 h.p. Rolls-Royce engine rather than the 160 h.p. Beardmore usual to the type. This made little difference to the airspeed of these 'flying birdcages' but the rate of climb was said to be much improved, 6,000 feet being reached in 10½ minutes.

Early in December the squadron was ordered to France and the administrative officers and ground staff embarked at Avonmouth on 9 December. However, they spent a week on board ship while the Navy searched for a U-boat believed to be lurking in the Bristol Channel.

The progress of the Fees was also slow; bad weather caused delays and left the pilots, each with a fitter as passenger, kicking their heels at Farnborough and other aerodromes in the south. Eventually the clouds cleared a little and they could take off to set course over the Channel and join the British Expeditionary Force. The first plane landed at St André aux Bois on 12 December, though by now some of the aircraft were so weather-beaten that they had to be left behind. In due course, the squadron was reassembled, the thirty-fifth RFC squadron to arrive in France.

It is recorded that Christmas was celebrated with 'the usual concerts, football matches and dinners'. On 22 January 1917, the squadron moved to Fienvilliers to join 9th (Headquarters) Wing commanded by Lt-Col C.L.N. Newall AM.[2]

Fienvilliers was a well-established aerodrome already occupied by No. 27 Squadron, flying Martinsyde 'Elephant' bombers. The village, situated at the junction of five roads on the way south to Amiens, housed Wing HQ as well as being the railhead for No. 2 Aeroplane Supply Depot and the repair depot, two very large establishments at nearby Candas.

Some of 57's personnel were housed in the village and on 27 January the CO authorized the Squadron Recording Officer (Adjutant) to pay M. Augustin Pion the sum of 15 francs for billeting allowances. A later chitty records another payment, this time for 15 francs 40 centimes in respect of billets for forty-four other ranks for seven nights, though Pion's neighbour, Nicholas Vimeux, received 9 francs for the undoubtedly superior accommodation of one officer for nine nights.

For three weeks, flying was handicapped by severe frost, midday temperatures reaching no more than 11°F, which caused difficulties in starting the water-cooled engines. Under the able control of Squadron Sergeant-Major Simpson the construction of canvas Bessoneau hangars proceeded apace and as these became available a solution to the problem was evolved. When an aeroplane landed the engine was drained of all but a little of the water. Each morning, with difficulty, sufficient water was heated and as each engine was started the aircraft was pulled backwards from the hangar with the propeller turning. This technique worked well and an average of 5½ hours was flown each day. However, if some of the troubles of the engine fitters were solved, more were created for the riggers and carpenters as tail-skids broke on the rock-hard ground.

The other ranks strength, consisting mainly of air mechanics, carpenters and sail-makers, had grown to 174 by 5 February but was still 46 below establishment. The rank of Air Mechanic, incidently, included batmen, cooks, orderly-room clerks, etc. being roughly equivalent to the Aircraftman of later years.

The frost began to ease by 11 February and there was great excitement as the squadron prepared for its first operation. Four aircraft were detailed for an 'offensive patrol and reconnaissance' south of the Arras salient.

Refuelling a BE2c, one of the squadron's first training aircraft (W. Waterhouse)

In the event, only two took off and these soon became parted. So it was that Major Pattinson and his observer, Lt Margoliouth, were alone as they crossed the lines and descended to investigate what they took to be a BE2c. This turned out to be an enemy Roland two-seater and as they realized their mistake they came under fire from three Albatros Scouts. Hardly had the combat started than Pattinson's Vickers gun jammed. His inexperienced colleague fought valiantly, expending seven drums of Lewis ammunition as they withdrew, though without much effect. On landing at Le Hameau thirty-seven bullet-holes were found in their aircraft, including the one in the engine water-jacket that had forced them to land. Meanwhile, the crew of the other plane had returned to base with little to report.

On 6 March the CO led 'C' Flight on a patrol and returned alone. The flight had been pounced upon by fifteen enemy scouts, resulting in the squadron's first casualties. Two aircraft had been forced down behind enemy lines and their crews captured. Another struggled back to a crash-landing in friendly territory, the airmen involved escaping unhurt. The pilot of the fourth, Lt W.F.W. Hills, was killed as his crippled plane crashed and his companion died soon after of a bullet wound.

Between operational flights, flying and gunnery practice continued. A favourite target was a pond near the aerodrome. Some 20 yards in diameter, it showed the 'fall of shot' much better than a conventional target, usually a discarded wing laid on the grass. A total of twenty-nine hours of training flights was reached by early March, considered to be very good for the time of the year.

A stray dog joined the squadron during the month and stayed throughout the summer, becoming a favourite with all. He was named Cappy after a Geordie pitman's dog in a song that had been performed with great success at the Christmas concert:

Engine service (W. Waterhouse)

Well deun, Cappy, famous au'd Cappy.
Cappy's the dog, Tallio, Tallio.

His special trick was to chase his tail, though if he managed to catch it he would stand with a look of complete bewilderment. His ancestry was obscure but it was generally agreed that it must include pointer and foxhound, enough to rank him among the famous '57 Varieties'!

When No. 55 Squadron arrived with their DH4s, Fienvilliers became a very busy station. By air, on 12 March, there was another arrival, the CO, RFC, Maj-Gen Sir Hugh Trenchard. Although suffering from the after-effects of a bout of bronchitis, he still insisted on keeping up his regular visits to the squadrons. (His despairing doctor told him that flying would either kill him or cure him.)

When he met 57 on this first occasion he promised that they would soon get plenty of fighting. He kept his word. Six days later he came again and told them of the value of their reconnaissance work and spoke of the German retreat on the Arras–Somme front, although the Battle of Arras proper did not begin until three weeks later. He also made mention of Allied air supremacy, which may well have provoked murmurs among his audience, for he was more than a few weeks out on that score.[3]

To an ever increasing degree Allied commanders relied on observations carried out by airmen, an extension of the role of the cavalry scout, whereas the Germans tended to use kite-balloons – 'Hildas' to the RFC. Generally, enemy planes maintained standing patrols high above their own lines and seldom ventured beyond No-Man's-Land. Eight of 57's Fees flew as far as Le Cateau on reconnaissance on 23 March, where they were attacked by a number of two-seaters. These they managed to shake off to reach the safety of Allied lines.

The air offensive in support of the Arras campaign began in early April but as the Allies advanced things were far from well with the Royal Flying Corps, facing as it did a foe with many advantages. The greatest of these were the Albatros DIs and DIIs, firing synchronized twin Spandau machine-guns through the propeller disc. No British planes at this time could hope to match the German machines for speed and handling, but squadrons such as 57 responded to continuous demands from HQ and whenever weather permitted their crews would be aloft, crossing the lines to where the Albatri – the RFC's plural – and *Eindekkers* waited in the sun.

The German Ace, Manfred von Richthofen, considered lone Fees easy game. On one April day he made three patrols, morning, midday and evening over the snow-covered trenches and on each occasion shot down one of the 'old lattice-tails', as he called them – although, like many other German pilots, he could never distinguish the type from the Vickers 'Gun-bus' of rather similar appearance.

Formerly of the King's Own Yorkshire Light Infantry, Lt N.C. Denison, the squadron's first Gunnery Officer, wrote a report after his release from prison camp. In it he told of von Richthofen's personal victories over two of 57's aircraft, which were sent down in flames. This was on 2 April, when Denison was flying with Capt Tomlinson, 'A' Flight Commander. While over Courcelles the patrol of three planes was attacked by a formation of eight Albatri led by the Baron. One of the Fees shot down an enemy fighter but immediately paid the penalty. Within seconds another Fee followed, but Tomlinson continued to fight. For six or seven minutes he and Denison used all the skills they could muster, shooting down two Germans, one of them, it turned out later, an Ace with eighteen victories. Eventually, Tomlinson fainted at the controls. Neither was hurt in the inevitable crash but the pilot died later of his wounds.

Lt Denison wrote of his admiration for Capt Tomlinson's conduct and told how this esteem was shared by von Richthofen's pilots when he met them immediately after being captured. The Baron later credited this victory to Leutnant Kreft.

On the night 5/6 April the first British night-bomber squadron, No. 100, took off from their base at Izel le Haneau and, in company with others, twice attacked the Baron's lair at Douai. Much damage was done but the enemy was not to be denied. The very next morning 57 lost a complete patrol of five aircraft, shot down, not by Albatri but by slow two-seaters. The FE was not a fighter and all the optimism and confidence of the Royal Aircraft Factory would not make it one.

The squadron lost another plane on 7 April, that of Lt Hamilton, which fell in flames. He managed to retain control by constantly changing hands on the hot joystick until, when almost on the ground, he and his gunner, Pte Snelling, bailed out without benefit of parachutes. Both escaped injury, though Hamilton suffered burns.

In the course of little more than a week the larger part of the squadron's flying personnel had become casualties. Swiftly, their places were taken by poorly trained youngsters almost straight from school, along with officers and, to an increasing degree, other ranks volunteering from field units.

The mention of Pte Snelling is the first reference to other rank aircrew with 57, but within a few weeks the classification 'Aerial Gunner, on Probation' was recorded. This offered 4s (20p) per day flying pay and – given survival – the chance to earn, after fifty hours of combat flying, the Observer's Badge, or 'Flying O' – (there was another, bawdier, name).

Douai was attacked again on the night of 7 April, but although these raids were tactical successes they afforded no respite. Rather, they led to the formation in due course of von Richthofen's famous 'Circus', the first of the mobile units whereby a convoy of special vehicles could lift a complete Jagdgeschwader and transport it overnight to a new field.

An FE2b, the type with which No. 57 first went to war (IWM Q57629)

Constantly in danger of attack, it seemed to the pilots of the Fees that all that could be done when caught alone, was to turn the ungainly biplane around and head for home, slowed by the prevailing west wind, while the man in the bath-tub of a front cockpit swung his Lewis gun from side to side, hoping for a shot at the pursuers. (Their alleged 'offensive' role meant that 57's Fees were not fitted with a second, rear-facing gun-mount, as was usual.)

Something had to be done and the pilots discussed the problem at great length. The solution was admirable in its directness. In future attacks the Fee was to turn and face the danger. The gunner was to remain still, firing only forwards so that his movements would not impair the pilot's freedom to manoeuvre and the aircraft would remain a stable gun platform for the Vickers gun on the top main-plane. The effect was instant and remarkable, at least in the short term. The casualty rate dropped for a week or two, as did the damage reports and, as if to prove the point, Lt Mears bagged an Albatros.

When, on 23 April, the First and Third Armies attacked on the Gavrelle–Croiselles front, Zero Hour was 04.45 hours. Observation for the artillery began at first light and finished at dusk, for the infantry was engaged in desperate fighting throughout the day.

Towards the end of the month HQ Wing was strengthened by the arrival of No. 56 (Fighter) Squadron. The incomparable Albert Ball was among their experienced leaders and although most of their pilots were unblooded it was hoped that their equipment, the new SE5, would prove the answer to the 'Fokker Scourge'. Trenchard was eager for the SEs to come to grips. A trap was laid and a flight of 57's Fees was to be the bait. Led by Lt Morice, they were to fly over Douai and Cambrai aerodromes to tempt von Richthofen and his men, while 56 waited high above.

Morice and his men played their part, the Baron duly took off to join battle, but of the SEs there was no sign. It transpired that the Germans had not risen to the bait. The 3rd, 4th, 11th and 33rd Jasta had combined to form Jagdgruppe 1 and today they were to fly together for the first time. Accordingly, Manfred von Richthofen delayed packing for a fortnight's home leave to lead the score of pilots, his younger brother Lothar among them, for the debut of the enhanced Circus; fate decreed that 57 should cross their path.

The usual tactics adopted by a formation of Fees when under attack was to form a circle, each crew covering the rear of the machine in front. With several guns able to come to bear on an enemy foolish enough to come within range, the impregnable 'ring of fire' would edge its way towards home and safety. Morice brought his flight into a circle and the Red Baron could only shake his fist and mouth insults in his frustration. Soon, however, the pilot of one of the Fees succumbed to temptation and broke formation to fire at a hostile machine.

The way was now open for the enemy. Within seconds two of 57's aircraft fell. Morice's observer, Lt Leathley, emptied two drums of Lewis ammunition at a pair of Fokkers but, even as one of these began to break up, von Richthofen dived in headlong attack. As he blazed away, bits flew off the Flt Ldr's Fee and the engine was hit, but somehow the airmen were untouched. With great skill, Morice managed to break away and head for home.

Three of their opponents continued to attack and, as was the custom in retreat, Leathley stood up to face the stern, slapping the pilot on the side of the head to indicate the direction of the next attack. In his excitement, he landed some of the slaps with uncalled-for enthusiasm. Struggling to keep control as the safety of the British lines drew nearer, with hot water from the leaking radiator pouring down his neck, the exasperated pilot responded with a right cross to the jaw and the observer subsided into his cockpit.

A minute later Morice put the battered machine down on the ground, finishing up in a shell hole by a gun battery. The two crawled from the wreckage to be met by an irate colonel who pointed out in forceful terms that they had smashed the only telescopic sight in France. He paused as he noticed their bedraggled appearance and added, 'I say, are you chaps alright?' They were, indeed, 'alright', apart from Leathley's hurt jaw and feelings. Lt Morice was awarded the Military Cross soon after this action. Back at base, they found that the remaining Fees had made good their escape when a flight of Sopwith Triplanes broke up the rest of the action.

By 29 April the weather had improved and while on patrol a flight of five of 57's aircraft came upon three of 56's SEs under attack by six Albatri and joined in. One of the enemy was shot down and the pilot was seen to fall from his cockpit. However, before the Germans left to join von Richthofen's larger formation one of the Fees crashed on the 'wrong' side of the trenches, and the crew members were taken prisoner.

Many a 'qualified' pilot arrived in France during this period with no more than ten solo flying hours in his logbook; by this time the life expectancy of a combat pilot on the Western Front was down to less than a fortnight. For 57, as for the RFC as a whole, the month was well named 'Bloody April' for it cost the squadron dear. In that month eight of their comrades were killed, four wounded and fifteen taken prisoner. The first few weeks in action had taken thirty-six of the unit's aircrew – exactly the established strength; thus was the phoenix tradition born and it was at this time that the emblem was adopted as an unofficial badge.

NOTES TO CHAPTER 1

1   As Air Vice-Marshal, Sir Philip Joubert de la Ferté became C-in-C Coastal Command in the Second World War.

2   An airman destined to be Chief of Air Staff by the outbreak of another world war.

3   In fairness to the General, his frequent talks to aircrews at this time showed that he was well aware of the many shortcomings of the planes they flew.

CHAPTER 2

Success and Victory

News came to the squadron early in May that their alleged offensive role was to be extended and on 5 May came confirmation that the Fees were to be replaced by DH4 bombers. After 'a settled routine of patrols and training' the Fees were gladly handed over to No. 25 Squadron and 57 began to convert to tractor aircraft. This training was to be carried out with what were considered suitable planes – none other than BE2cs, the old Quirks.

A month was allotted for the work and according to one account this was none too long, some of the progress being 'rather poor'. At the end of May the unit moved to Droglandt with some of the new bombers. This move seems to have been ill-considered as the aerodrome was quite inadequate for the comparatively large and heavy machines. Even so, pilots who made good progress soon found themselves detailed for photographic reconnaissance missions.

The DH4 has been called 'the best single-engined bomber of the war' and must have made life very different for the crews (and perhaps a little more likely), though some complained of the oil and smoke that blew back from the engine and longed for the 'ventilation arrangements' of the old pushers. Though equipped with basically the same engine, the Rolls-Royce Eagle, the performance was greatly enhanced with a top speed of 125 m.p.h. instead of 90, and the ability to reach 16,700 feet with one 230 lb bomb or two 112 lb bombs.

The pilot's Vickers machine-gun was synchronized so as to fire through the propeller disc and in the rear cockpit the Lewis gun was mounted on a Scarff Ring, giving immensely better handling and an increased firing arc. Yet another innovation was the introduction of oxygen equipment and 57 was among the first squadrons to experience the benefits of breathing oxygen in both reconnaissance and bombing operations at the higher altitudes now attainable.

The first bombing raid was planned for 14 June but, because of cloud, was aborted – the term was already in use in this context. The next day, however, several 20 lb bombs were dropped on Reckem aerodrome and another raid was carried out on the aerodrome at Handzaeme, some 15 miles behind the enemy lines. These raids were completed without loss but it was the Droglandt airfield that won in the end. As Lt Morice recorded later, 'the crashery rather reduced our efficiency, only three machines being serviceable at one time, the rest in ruins'.

I joined 57 Squadron on April 11th 1917. We were then stationed at Fienvilliers with F.E.2.B. machines, the Flight Commanders were then A Flight, Lt Harken* B Flight, Capt MacNaughton C Flight, Lt Pope*.

We were doing line patrols and bomb raids escorts during this time with occasionally an offensive patrol. We were having casualties at this time losing two Flight Commanders Capt Tomlinson, A Flight, Capt Platt C Flight just before I arrived, this was due to Capt Richthovens Circus.

I remember one offensive patrol on April 30th our instructions were to sit over Douai and Cambrai aerodromes and get the Huns off the ground, there was a pretty stiff westerly wind which was much against the old F.E. and made Archie very accuate (sic). Having arrived

*Promoted Captains soon after this.

de Havilland DH4, the unit's first 'real' bomber (IWM Q68130)

over Donai (*sic*) in good formation we were pounced on by the Circus which seemed to appear from no where, the scrap developed into a dog fight in which my observer got one HA down, but we were immediately badly holed in the raditor (*sic*) and water jackets of the engine by I believe Richthoven himself, with boiling water down my neck I thought it time to get home I put my nose down and headed towards home with 3 HA after me. They kept diving one after each other from all directions, each time they dived my observer who was watching my tail kept hitting me on the side of my head the way they were diving in order to make me turn in that direction to try and drive them off. I think the thought of landing in Germany must have been troubling my observer, I know it was me because each time he struck me was harder that the last till I could not stand it any longer, so I stood up and hit him back unfortunately placing him Hors de Combat for the rest of the trip, I cannot mention names as perhaps my observer may not like it. We eventually crashed into a shell hole behind the front line at Rochlincourt just off of Arras.

My observer and I are still quite friendly, although I got another, and he took a different pilot.

Nothing much of note took place after this, until about the end of May we were ordered to get rid of our F.E.s as we were to have D.H.4s. For nearly a month we practised on tractor machines sometimes successfully and sometimes not, till with a complete squadron of D.H.4s we moved to Drogland aerodrome. I cannot say that this move was a success as the aerodrome was small and awkward for big machines. We carried on with Photographic and bombing raids until the Crashery rather reduced our efficiency, only 3 machines being serviceable at one time, the rest in ruins.

I think No. 10 Naval Squadron who were on the same aerodrome were glad to see the last of us, as on one occasion one of our pilots quietly flew through one of their sheds wrecking 3 Triplanes, we were then moved to Boisdinghem.

I was promoted Flight Commander in July and after about two months quite successful work at Boisdinghem, I left for Home Establishment in September.

(signed) C.S. Morice[1]
Major MC RAF

HQ South Western Area
Salisbury
11/4/19[2]

The result was a move to Boisdinghem, west of St Omer, and 57 arrived there on 27 June. This aerodrome was described, perhaps with tongue in cheek, as 'good, apart from some depressions 18 inches deep by 15 feet in diameter' – probably inadequately filled shell holes of earlier battles.

By now the squadron was equipped with its full complement of eighteen DHs, painted dark khaki-green with the squadron identification mark, a white disc aft of the RFC roundel. It was ready to join battle on the Ypres Sector and at the beginning of July was allotted to 22nd Wing, V Brigade, and formally designated a Day Bomber Squadron, though still tasked with a great deal of photographic reconnaissance work.

On 5 July the first bombing operation involving six planes took off but the raid was aborted. On returning, Lt Erlebach tore the undercarriage from his machine on the bank of a sunken road. Some of the 20 lb bombs aboard exploded and the pilot was killed. His observer, Lt Trotter, was injured in a rescue attempt. Erlebach was one of the few on the squadron to have survived the bitter fighting with the Fees and his loss was keenly felt.

A curious report tells that, on 7 July, 'lead objects were dropped on Heulard Courtrai, with good results and photographs'. Fifteen of the enemy attacked the main formation but were driven off, losing two of their comrades for their pains. A bomber that strayed from the main formation also shot down an enemy machine.

On some of their early bombing raids 57 Squadron was escorted by Sopwith Triplanes flown by 'Naval Ten' and other squadrons of the Royal Naval Air Service based in the Pas de Calais, behind the Northern Sector. The Navy achieved a high measure of success with the 'Tripehounds' and these fast and highly manoeuvrable machines quickly gained the respect of the enemy (and received the ultimate accolade from Antony Fokker when he based the design of his *Dreidekker* on them).

Success began to attend the efforts of the squadron more regularly through the summer of 1917. The deeds of one particular day are recorded at length and seem worth quoting in full:

July 27th was a day of great events. After a successful dawn reconnaissance, operations were impossible until afternoon when two hostile aerodromes were attacked by five machines each. Results of bombing were mainly unobserved, although two 112 lb bombs were seen to burst in a field about 150 yards clear of Bissegem aerodrome.

When returning from the objective, Captain Minot, leading the formation of five machines, dived at three machines which were a few hundred feet below near Houthulst Forest. Some twenty Albatros Scouts which were to the west of the forest attacked the formation and a desperate fight ensued at 13,000 feet. Captain Minot brought down two of the enemy with his front gun and Lieutenant Britton accounted for another and was slightly wounded below the knee. Lieutenant Hall shot one machine down out of control but unfortunately Lieutenant Pizey's gun jambed (*sic*). This officer was mortally wounded through the head and died shortly after landing at La Louie aerodrome, near Poperringhe. Lieutenants Irwin and Leete accounted for one machine each, the pilot being wounded in the big toe,[3] but regaining his aerodrome safely. Lieut. Roadley shot down a seventh scout with his front gun and was fortunate to come safely out of action as his engine gave trouble whilst he was still engaged. Lieut. O'Beirne's machine was disabled and his observer, Lieut. Rayner, killed in the course of the fight. When making a forced landing with damaged controls near the Belgian coast, the machine hit a tree and the pilot was so severely injured that he died shortly after being taken to hospital.

Few hostile machines were sighted by the formation led by Captain Boake, but a single machine manoeuvring for position was shot down out of control at 350 yards range by Lieutenant Godwin, flying with Lieutenant Hutcheson. This was the first occasion on which two Lewis guns, mounted side by side were used in combat on a machine of 57 Squadron.

Besides the two bombing raids and the dawn reconnaissance two successful sets of photographs were taken by Lieutenant Pym, flying with Lieutenant Morice and Lieutenant Bullock with Lieutenant Cooke.

An evening reconnaissance completed the day's work.

The squadron received a message of congratulations from General Trenchard soon after its 'day of great events'. The following day was also eventful, four enemy machines being shot down, but sadly, Lt Minot was killed in this action.

A total of eighteen German aircraft were destroyed by 57 Squadron through July for the loss of six of their own, though, sadly, ten of their colleagues were killed.

An innovation at this time was the introduction of negative lens bomb sights. The sight took the form of a plywood box set into the floor of the aircraft. A lens, several inches square, was fixed in the top, with cross-rods, adjustable for height and speed, fitted in the bottom.

Army HQ were now demanding oblique photographs for their artillery work and by August, cameras with long focal-length lenses had become the fashion. These could produce, from 18,000 feet, a print showing an area 500 yards by 400 yards, which helped the squadron maintain its acknowledged proficiency in support of the artillery. The clarity, however, was often marred by smoke and the evil clouds of poison gas.

No. 1 Aircraft Supply Depot, Clairmarais, was a twenty-minute ride from Boisdinghem, rattling over the pavé road by tender or motor-bike, and 'Collected new aircraft from No. 1 ASD' was a fairly frequent logbook entry, especially for new pilots, for work with the DH4s was not without mishaps. Besides enemy scouts and 'Archie' – anti-aircraft fire – other hazards faced the aviators. Lts Goodyear and Martin were killed when their machine received a direct hit from a field-gun shell. Such occurrences were by no means rare, for the shells of the heavy guns often reached 2,000 feet, while howitzers were set at such an angle that the projectile was thrown up to 7,000 feet, where crews often saw one 'hovering' at the top of its trajectory.

Another regular task for the pilots was the flight-testing of aircraft and one or more of these flights would take place almost every day. In the back seat often sat the senior NCO of the section concerned, a practice still recognized as an effective form of quality control! Generally, the comment recorded after landing was 'Satis.' though sometimes magneto or carburettor trouble would be noted. In the case of a test after rigging, a comment such as 'Tail heavy' might appear. Interestingly, the categorizations 'S' or 'U/S' were already in use to denote aircraft serviceability.

On 16 August the squadron dropped the remarkable total of 3,600 lb of bombs on railway sidings and the aerodromes at Heulard and Reckem, as well as taking photographs of the bombing objectives and of part of the counter-battery area – the target area for the various gun batteries by whom they were employed.

The next day, Maj Joy and Lt Leathley (now parted from Morice by mutual consent) equalled the record of Capt Minot and Lt Britton by downing three enemy planes in one day, but 21 August saw the loss of the first DH engaged on reconnaissance work. Sgt Boucher and Air Mechanic Harmston received wounds, to which the latter succumbed. The airmen had flown together for some weeks in a successful partnership and on this last operation had shot down a 'hostile'.

While flying over cloud one day Lts Hood and McDaniel were amazed to see the lozenge-patterned wings of a twin-engined Gotha bomber emerging from the murk below. Quickly overcoming their surprise they poured bullets into the giant and sent it crashing to the ground. During August no fewer than twenty-one of the enemy had fallen to 57's guns but six of their own aircraft had been lost. On a lighter note, another report in September recorded that 'casualties were very heavy' in an encounter of a different kind when 57 beat their neighbours of 55 Squadron by two tries to nil at rugby!

The Battle of the Menin Ridge Road took place between 20 and 25 September and 57 was among the twenty-five squadrons involved. Stationed on the right flank of the Fifth Army front, they were responsible for keeping watch on enemy movements throughout the day, reporting their sightings by dropping messages on the Army report centre. The patrols were carried out from 6–8,000 feet but the pilots were ordered to descend to low level fifteen minutes before they were due to return to search out and attack any German reinforcements on the move.

Seven of the heaviest bombs that the DH4 could carry – 230-pounders – were dropped on enemy billets in the village of Hooglede on 24 and 25 September, and similar targets 'received attention' on the following day, despite bad weather.

Rain and low cloud continued through much of October, adding to the misery of the poor devils committed to live, and probably die, in the endless mud and green-slimed shell holes below the airmen who were supporting a series of British pushes. These were to lead to the first Battle of Passchendaele on 12 October and the second on 26 October. On one of these patrols three machines were used and the Operations Record Book mentions this as 'an occasion of note', for almost the whole of the counter-battery area was covered by 144 exposures with an E-Type camera.

The busiest day the RFC had ever seen, 27 October, saw 57 well involved, bombing Roulers as well as carrying out their artillery support work. High winds hampered the latter: '70 mph at over 15,000 feet made work very difficult.'

On 4 November, just before the Battle of Cambrai, command of the squadron was transferred to Maj C.I.A. Hiatt MC and shortly after this more congratulations were received from Army Command, this time for the bombing of Roulers.

Later in the month, 57 moved once again, their destination Ste Marie Cappel, south of Cassel and near the Belgian border. Here Nos 20 and 60 Squadrons were operating with Bristol Fighters and SEs respectively and 57 were to take over the photographic work of the sector from No. 45 Squadron. Under the command of Maj A.T. Harris[4] and recently equipped with the new Sopwith Camel Fighters, 45 Squadron were on their way to the Italian front. The newcomers were happy to inherit the Nissen huts, newly built to replace the bell-tents, as well as the fine new Church Army Reading Room where other ranks might spend a leisure hour.

Among odd papers in the archives is a request from HQ for a list of those Observers with more than five months' service in the field. Dated 14 December, it is a 'Nil Return'.

In the short days of December, with weather often unfit for flying, Maj Hiatt introduced a programme of 'Winter Training'. The regular syllabus for each day might see the crews attending talks on such matters as navigation and map-reading followed by practical work with the camera-gun. At 11.45, a session of physical training; after lunch, drill alternated with football. At dusk, more lectures covering a variety of subjects from rigging and oxygen sets to the Vickers gun. One evening, a corporal spoke on the Camera Obscura and the CO's evening summary at 7.15 rounded off a pretty full day.

The squadron was airborne early on New Year's Day 1918, and Bissegem aerodrome was attacked once again. An interesting feature of this raid was that the bombs were dropped at a signal from the leader, a method that became common practice in the Second World War.

The pattern for the following months was well set. Each day, as weather allowed, the bombers would set off for a target, often many miles behind the enemy lines. The bomb load would consist of eight 20 lb Cooper bombs, two 112 lb, or sometimes a single 230-pounder. On each flight the crews were expected to bring back reports of their observations – locomotives in steam, numbers and types of vehicles on the road and so on. In addition, every day one or two planes would set off to photograph the counter-battery area. Each camera-load of eighteen exposures had to be delivered to Army HQ – the trip to Fienvilliers and return to St Marie was considerably longer than the operation flight.

Casualties on the squadron were now lower than they had been but still replacements were needed. These came from many sources, from famous regiments such as the Black Watch as well as lesser-known units. Lt Margerison transferred to the world of aviation from the unlikely background of the 1/1st Huntingdonshire Cyclist Battalion but as the war dragged on experienced junior officers became too scarce to release from the field units and, like most squadrons, 57 soon had a number of Canadians on the nominal roll.

On 31 March the Germans made their last throw, hurling themselves forward to break through the British Fifth Army sector. The BEF reeled under the onslaught and 'Backs to the wall!' was the desperate call from HQ. No. 57 Squadron, by now attached to Second Brigade, played their full part, attacking Menin, Courtrai, Roulers and other targets as the enemy overran them, and bombing Lille station twice on 23 March.

The massed German troops were a target not to be ignored and on 26 March the squadron was one of four detached to reinforce First Brigade with low-flying attacks on the columns of enemy infantry as they breached the Third Army front. In all, thirty-seven squadrons were engaged in these counter-measures and a total of 250,000 rounds was fired from the air that day – one of 57's aircraft loosed off 900 rounds on a single sortie. Throughout the morning, the Germans poured through the gap they had forced in the British lines but by evening the critical situation was under control.

At the end of March the squadron moved to Le Quesnoy, four miles from the Belgian border, taking with them a newly received signal of congratulations for the bombing of the ammunition dump at Bapaume on 27 of that month. One may have a mental picture of an enormous explosion, but the signal was, to say the least, premature. Once, twice, sometimes even three times a day up to 30 June, 57 Squadron hammered away at this target, which was in fact a huge supply of Allied ammunition abandoned when the enemy overran Bapaume on 17 March.

The Royal Air Force was formed on 1 April and Capt F. McD. Turner MC and Lt Leach celebrated the occasion by shooting down two enemy scouts. While on a photographic mission they were attacked by five triplanes; they quickly despatched one of these in flames but in a minute or two the battle was joined by ten other hostiles. A drum of Lewis 'ammo' was emptied into one of the newcomers at 100 yards and it fell apart. The two made good their escape and, indeed, claimed another victim within a few days. Lt Leach was awarded the MC a week later, an occasion worthy of what was known as a 'jolly good drunk'.

The Battle of Vimy Ridge, which culminated in the capture of 10,000 Germans, began amid snow and rain, but fine weather on 12 April enabled the Service to drop a greater tonnage of bombs and to expose more photographic plates than on any other day since the war began.

On 10 June, during a raid on the Bapaume dump, Lt C.W. Peckham and Sgt J. Grant were attacked by eight Fokker Triplanes. Grant loosed a burst at the first of these, sending it down in flames, but the remaining 'Trips' headed them off, compelling Peckham to fly north. One opened fire from below but Peckham dived on it. After firing eighty rounds into it he saw it crash before he made good his own escape.

Capt A. McGregor was recommended for the MC in June, but became the first officer on the squadron to receive the Distinguished Flying Cross on the institution of this decoration on 23 June.

As the assault on the Bapaume dump neared its close, Lt A.D.R. Jones and Sgt J.T. Wood claimed another victim and on 25 June Lt Brown and Sgt Shepstone came back with a fine tale to tell. They had fallen out of combat as bullets riddled the gravity tank and set it on fire. Down they went as a 'flamer' until, suddenly, the fire went out. By now they were down to 5,000 feet but they climbed back to 19,000 feet, recrossed the lines and resumed their photographic task.

By mid-July, having suffered 800,000 casualties, the Germans faltered and finally their offensive was abandoned.

In the summer, 57 Squadron, now under the command of Maj G.C. Bailey DSO, found themselves located at Hesdin, between Montreuil and St Pol. Their work continued, even increased, as the BEF gathered themselves to recover lost ground in what proved to be the final assaults. The French counter-offensive began on 5 July.

On 8 August, ten of the DHs successfully attacked Moislains aerodrome, situated to the north of the Somme. Capt McD. Turner, OC 'A' Flight, led the raid and he and Lt Musgrave accounted for an enemy plane. Sgt Denis Edgley, who celebrated his nineteenth birthday during the month, was a pilot at the time and recalled the operation:

After crossing the lines at around 10,000 feet we dived headlong down and bombed and machine-gunned the hangars and grounded planes from a few hundred feet in the course of a hurly-burly dog-fight with enemy fighters which took off in defence as they saw us descending. What a scrap! In the midst of it, Lieutenant Brown, while busy machine-gunning the hangars from little more than nought feet, had his engine disabled by enemy fire and actually landed on their airfield! I can't imagine what the reception committee said to him!

The second week of August brought a fine spell and this led to the fiercest air fighting of the war. The RAF claimed 177 aircraft destroyed and 90 sent down out of control, for the loss of 90. The enemy was now in retreat and much of the work of the day-bombers was concentrated on the destruction of the bridges over the Somme to impede the withdrawal. No. 57 Squadron was tasked with the bombing of the bridge at Peronne on 9 August and two flights took off at 07.00 hours. Their escort of five Bristol Fighters from No. 11 Squadron became detached when attacked by eight Fokkers and the leader of the bombers decided against continuing the raid on the bridge as more 'hostiles' were seen approaching. Instead, they turned their attention to the railway sidings at nearby Vinstead and, although fighters assailed them as they made their run at 12,000 feet, the bombs were dropped on target and all the planes returned safely.

The end result of this short campaign against the bridges was successful in an unexpected way. In fact, none was damaged to any degree but, such was their importance to the Germans, that they were obliged to defend them at all costs and lost many of their best pilots in so doing.

Heading for base from another raid on 14 August, a formation of 57's aircraft came under fire from enemy scouts. One of these got on the tail of Capt McGregor and was promptly shot

The officers of No. 57 Squadron at Le Quesnoy, France, in the spring of 1918. The CO, Major Hiatt, is seated in the centre of the front row. On his right is Captain Stokes, 'B' Flight Commander; to his left, Major Binning. Behind Binning, wearing the bonnet of the Argyle & Sutherlands, stands Captain MacGregor, 'A' Flight Commander (D. Edgley)

down by his observer, Lt J.F.D. Tanqueray, the pilot being seen to bail out with a parachute just before his machine caught fire. Sgt Grant, observer with a Canadian pilot, Lt E.M. Coles, also shot down a hostile machine which had fastened onto their tail and again the pilot was seen to descend 'in' a parachute, as it was phrased at the time.[5] Lts Anderson and Stevens also came under close attack in this engagement and they too had success, for smoke was seen coming from their opponent's aircraft as it fell and the wings broke off as it reached the ground.

All the fighting did not end in 57's favour, however, for they lost two of their aircraft during a raid on the railway station at Ytres.

At the end of August Capt Turner MC was awarded the DFC but his notable career with the squadron came to an abrupt end as he side-slipped in to land at Hesdin. Apparently, his left wing-tip caught one of the sawn-off trees by the boundary road and the plane cartwheeled into the field, ending with its tail in the air and back broken. The unfortunate pilot was extracted with some difficulty and survived, though with severe facial injuries.

During bombing operations on 1 September two formations from 57 came under fire from German scouts, and again successful engagements followed. Sgts Edgley and Sandison set fire to one hostile machine and drove another down out of control. Coles and Grant again had success, as did Lts F.C. Thornton and F.C. Craig. During the same week, Thornton attained another victory, this time in the company of Lt W.H. Thornton. It may be that these two were brothers. Sgt Edgley could not say: 'Social relations between flying sergeants and the officers were virtually nil.'

Despite this, there could have been little wrong with the working relationship. Sgt Grant's guns were in action again some days later when, flying with Capt McGregor, he set fire to a Fokker. The pilot was seen to jump out, apparently *without* a parachute. A few days later Grant was awarded the Distinguished Flying Medal, the squadron's first, followed by a 'home posting', his personal 'score' standing at twelve aircraft destroyed.

Later in the month, with scarcely a pause in the action, the unit moved to Vert Galand. Backing up the assault on the Hindenburg Line, they bombed targets at Rumilly and various German HQ, such as that at Awoingt, south-east of Cambrai. As the Allies advanced, so the squadrons followed, ever eastward. Just before the final push that broke the Hindenburg Line, 57 moved to Mory, a mile or two north of Bapaume. The campaign reached its successful conclusion on 8 October and was followed by the second Battle of Le Cateau. Both Le Cateau and Cambrai were cleared of the enemy by 10 October but for another month the Germans received no respite. Every day 57 joined in with high-level bombing, giving their invaluable help to the field-guns thundering below.

Still, too, enemy aircraft fell to the guns of Lt Newman, flying with Lts Pernet and Wilkinson on successive days and Sgt Mason, observer with Lt Pym. The last crew to claim victory was Lts Timson and Woodhouse, on an operation led by their 'B' Flight Commander, Capt Stokes.

But even in the last few weeks the squadron suffered losses. Capt Colville-Jones MC joined them on 30 October and was killed in action five days later. Capt Stoke's aircraft was hit by anti-aircraft fire and he died of his wounds, a prisoner. The observer aboard another plane hit by 'Archie', Sgt Sidney Tidey, was struck by a shrapnel fragment, which lodged in his brain. However, he lived to tell the tale – and did, sixty years later! Sgt Edgley finished the war in a clearing station at Bapaume, a casualty of a different kind. On his way to an interview following his application for a commission, he fell foul of the influenza epidemic that swept Europe and caused more deaths than the four years of fighting.

The aircraft flew on to yet another base on 9 November and it was from Beauvois that they made what were to be their last operations of the war. At 09.30 hours they set course for the 'railway triangle' at Marchienne au Pont, which they bombed from 11,000 feet, returning for a similar attack in the afternoon.

The squadron diarist could hardly have seen the end of the bloodiest war in history as a 'non-event', but for 11 November 1918 the Operations Record Book contains the brief entry: 'Nothing to report'! Perhaps he decided that it was not the day for paperwork, for doubtless, while the aeroplanes stood idle, the squadron members celebrated as best they could when the news of the Armistice came through.

Soon after, a summary of the squadron's achievements was drawn up showing that 285 tons of bombs had been dropped. On the 196 reconnaissance flights they had exposed over 22,000 photographic plates. Aircraft losses do not appear to have been recorded but the squadron suffered 104 fatal casualties. The destruction of 166 enemy planes was officially confirmed and a list of best 'shots' among the pilots (only) is headed by Capt Green, with nine victories to his credit. The list is long, though a minimum 'score' of four was necessary for inclusion. In less than two years, the squadron members had been awarded nine Military Crosses, three Distinguished Flying Crosses, two Military Medals, two Distinguished Flying Medals, two Meritorious Service Medals and a Croix de Guerre.

There were no targets left. No. 57 Squadron returned to Vert Galand for a couple of days, then on 24 November went on to Spy, near Mons, there to briefed for their new role as an Army Post Service. On 12 December the first of many mail-carrying flights took place, a 45-minute trip to Spa, where a unit of the squadron was eventually detached. Other runs were initiated to Valenciennes and so on, and on 10 January 1919, a regular daily route, Spy–Cologne–Morville, was opened. In time Morville became the major base for the squadron as their service expanded to include other destinations and small detachments were posted to various Belgian and French sites such as Franc Waret, Lez Bruyeres, Nivelles and Marquise.

Though the service ran smoothly as a rule, on 20 March Lt Smith was killed when his aircraft crashed on the return leg of the Cologne shuttle. (By now, pilots were usually flying solo on these eighty-minute flights so that the maximum capacity could be given over to cargo.)

In July the squadron was re-equipped with the fine DH9A. It had been designed as a bomber but during the 1920s it became the trailblazer and workhorse for many of the world's air-mail services, not least the United States Post Office.

An efficient service with good equipment was not enough, however, and the writing was on the wall. No. 57 Squadron worked on until August then returned to Blighty to be stood down. The Royal Air Force, little more than a year old, was being decimated. In the year that followed the end of the war, 90 per cent of the 317,000 officers, other ranks and airwomen were discharged. Aeroplanes went for scrap by the thousand and brand-new engines, still in their crates fetched £10 apiece. Airframes were broken up and many a set of main-planes that had never shone in the clouds ended its days as the walls of allotment tool-sheds.

No. 57 Squadron was disbanded at South Carlton, Nottinghamshire on 31 December 1919. Of 400 squadrons, only 12 remained.

NOTES TO CHAPTER 2

1   As the Allies advanced in 1944, Group Captain 'Tim' Morice, DSO, MC, took his wing of tank-busting Typhoons into Douai, making sure that his machine was parked exactly where the infamous Fokker had once stood.

2   PRO Ref AIR 1/173 HM03474.

3   Some years ago, after beginning this task, I noticed a headline in a local newspaper: 'How the Red Baron Shot my Big Toe!' Enquiries soon led to chats (over a dram) with a grand old man, still with a dry Scottish sense of humour though by then ninety. I left after my first visit with a carefully treasured copy of *Popular Flying*, July 1934. Written on the cover in a child's hand: 'Uncle Angus's Story'. It was headed: My Most Thrilling Flight. By A.C.S. Irwin (late RFC) (See Appendix B)

4   In February 1942, Maj A.T. Harris, by now an Air Chief Marshal, became AOC-in-C Bomber Command.

5   By mid-1918 many German airmen were wearing parachutes while, for various reasons, British airmen, with the exception of balloon observers, were denied these aids.

CHAPTER 3
Rebirth, 1931

Though the initial cutbacks to the service were violent, by the early 1920s the 'Hawks' of the day, Lord Trenchard among them, were in some ascendancy over the 'Doves'. However, they could never beat the Treasury; the RAF's average allocation from a meagre defence budget never exceeded 17 per cent until an astonishing leap to 40 per cent in 1938.

The size of Britain's defences was founded upon the 'Ten Year Rule', the theory that none of the major powers would be able to find sufficient manpower, will-power or wealth to wage war again in a lesser period. This reasonable line of thought, however, was subject to annual review, resulting in an extension each time for a further twelve months and this continued into the 1930s.

As the new decade opened, the British public was becoming more and more air-minded (to use the newly coined phrase), and the Royal Air Force already held a place in the hearts of the nation. The annual display at Hendon aerodrome in the summer of 1931 attracted a massive 175,000 spectators. They came from far and wide to be thrilled, and were not disappointed. The 'Air Defence of Great Britain' became the maxim and soon the formation of an air arm of that name (ADGB) was put in hand.[1] Expansion was rapid, on paper at any rate, and squadron numbers soon began to come out of cold storage.

So, on 20 October 1931, No. 57 (Day Bomber) Squadron was re-formed at Netheravon, Wiltshire, along with No. 18 Squadron, and both were quickly absorbed into ADGB as part of the Wessex Bombing Area. The Commanding Officer of the new-born squadron was Sqn Ldr H.G. Bowen MBE and his initial complement comprised eleven officers and eighty-seven men, including six airmen pilots. The equipment allocated to the two squadrons was the Hawker Hart powered by the Rolls-Royce 'Kestrel 1B'. The Hart was capable of 180 m.p.h. with a bomb load of 520 lb and, although some 70 miles an hour faster than 57's last combat aircraft, the DH4, was in fact smaller by several feet, carried only twice the 'pay-load' and still relied for defence on just a couple of .303 guns. Nevertheless, the Hart was a fine plane for its time and was faster than most of its contemporary single-seat biplane fighters.

The first flight with the new aircraft took place on 15 November when the CO took off with Cpl Goffe of No. 13 Squadron in the rear cockpit – his qualifications for the ride being his service with 57 as an observer during the war. A programme of training flights was soon in hand, the earliest consisting of affiliation exercises with the Bristol Bulldogs of No. 3 Squadron. By the year's end squadron strength had increased to 19 officers and 131 men, and with 12 aircraft they could muster two flights – 'HQ' and 'A'.

By 07.00 hours each morning, six days a week, the station's civilian workers would be at their place of work and at 4.30 p.m. they would stream from the camp on cycles or run for the bus along with the ORs who lived out. The hangar doors would be closed on time unless night-flying had been laid on to give experience to pilots and observers, or perhaps, for the benefit of the Army's searchlight and listening post crews. Airmen marched to the dining-hall for tea, some to reappear later in their walking-out dress of 'best blue', complete with cane and puttees, the circulation-stopping 'twirly-trousers'.

In June 1932 57 Squadron took part in their first RAF display at Hendon, ten aircraft rehearsing for several days before the event. The unit moved north on 18 July for the summer

Sqn Ldr H.E. Bowen MBE, with officers of the newly re-formed No. 57 (Day Bomber) Squadron, Netheravon, 1931 (W. Yandall)

camp and were joined by crews from the Reserve. They camped at North Coates Fitties, near Grimsby, spending their time on bombing exercises and air-firing – the period was made particularly notable in that not a drop of rain fell for the whole six weeks. Together, 18 and 57 Squadrons moved to Upper Heyford on 5 September 1932, and this was to be their home for the next seven years.

In January 1933 57 had a change of CO, when Sqn Ldr Trott OBE MC assumed command. Throughout the spring the two squadrons combined in their training and a 'Wing Drill' was successfully carried out at Andover as a rehearsal for the annual Hendon event. The real thing, however, was ruined by the weather which also caused the cancellation of an exercise with the Observer Corps, planned for July.

The move up north for the 1933 summer camp provided the opportunity for a mobilization exercise and the ground crews bivouacked at Cardington and Grantham en route for North Coates. The journey back was made in just one day, seen as something of an achievement, involving as it did a considerable convoy of vehicles on a 150-mile trip.

A new arrival in February 1934 was another CO, Sqn Ldr F.W. Walder DSC AFC. He was a former naval airman and came in time to supervise preparations for an exercise with a nautical flavour. Exercise Centurion to take place in the autumn would involve the dive-bombing of targets at sea.

May of that year saw the first Empire Air Day when dozens of aerodromes were thrown open to the public. The venture was a great success and became an annual event, benefiting the Royal Air Force Benevolent Fund by many thousands of pounds. Hangars and workshops, dining-halls

No. 57 Squadron at Upper Heyford in 1933 commanded by Sqn Ldr Trott OBE MC (W. Yandall)

and armouries were eagerly inspected by the local populace and many a seed was sown in receptive schoolboy minds. Throughout the afternoon the packed enclosures would be white with upturned faces – was the weather always fine? V-formations of chequered Siskins performed neat loops and rolls, coloured streamers showing the chains that linked the three aircraft together. Some suspected that the chains were tied on with string but that took nothing from the spectacle, for the string was never broken.

Next came the Bristol Bulldogs, bursting toy balloons with their propellers, then Vickers Virginia heavy bombers would make their stately approach, the parachutists on the wings ready to pull off at the right moment. Finally, the Harts would perform their party piece, attacking a timber and canvas 'native fort'. Nobody cared if the bangs and puffs of smoke failed to synchronize with the flour-bag 'bombs'. For some reason, dinner-plates were attached to the walls as targets. One of these would survive unscathed through countless machine-gun bursts until, as an armoured car approached to mop up survivors, a cocoa-stained 'fuzzy-wuzzy' in PT shorts dashed out to break that last plate with a hammer. The rifle drill ended, the winner of the height-guessing competition was announced and after the station band had played *The King*, everyone went home happy. Britain was in good hands.

The public may have been naive to a certain extent but the RAF's biplanes and armoured cars had long performed sterling service in the Middle East. Enthusiasm and good training could make up for much that was lacking in terms of equipment while some of the best aircraft designers in the world were being encouraged, albeit somewhat belatedly, to apply themselves to the task of producing planes worthy of the Service.

The squadron had a further exercise in public relations in May, when they flew north for the

The Hawker Hart, typical of the warplanes of the thirties (IWM ATP8882c)

inauguration of the Amsterdam to Hull route of the Royal Dutch Airline (KLM). After a fine lunch in the clubroom of the Hull Flying Club, they repaid their hosts with a flying display. Nos 18 and 57 Squadrons again appeared in the Hendon Display, their 1934 show taking the form of a formation-changing demonstration with Nos 600 and 601 Squadrons, Aux. AF.

Despite hold-ups while contractors fitted electro-magnetic bomb release gear to the Harts, 595 hours were flown through the summer. Much of this was taken up with bombing practice from 20,000 feet and the season finished with a month under canvas at Ford, near Arundel, while the dive-bombing exercises took place, using HMS *Centurion*,[2] a battleship under radio-control from HM Destroyer *Skikari*, as a target.

In accordance with an Air Ministry Order, the squadron's twenty-four Riggers and Fitters were posted out on 1 January 1935, to be replaced by twelve Fitters II and twelve Fitters' Mates. This had the effect of depriving the squadron of its trained, if part-time, air gunners, but the deficit was made good later when a dozen trained air gunners were brought in.

The Royal Air Force celebrated the Silver Jubilee of King George V with a Royal Review on 6 July and after His Majesty's Inspection at Mildenhall, 57 Squadron led No. 2 Flight, Bomber Group, in the fly-past over Duxford, 356 aircraft being involved in the whole event.

The expansion of the Service continued at an ever-increasing rate and on 16 March 1936, 57's 'C' Flight became the nucleus of the re-forming No. 218 Squadron, leaving them with two flights of six aircraft each.

The Armament Officers' Trophy had been awarded since 1930 for annual competition between the air gunners and air bombers of the day-bombing squadrons of ADGB. As in all

Service contests, competition for 'The Cock', as it was known, was fierce and it was a great day for the squadron when they won it for the first time in the spring of 1936. It turned out to be one of the last exercises with the Harts, for in May they re-equipped with Hawker Hinds, making their first appearance with the new type at Upper Heyford's Empire Air Day.

Very similar to the Hart in looks, the Hind was much improved in performance, with a ceiling of 26,450 feet. However, it still carried its 500 lb bomb load slung under the fabric-covered wings, and could only be seen as an interim type awaiting the advent of the projected stressed-skin monoplanes. The first exercise with the new type was in cooperation with the Observer Corps and involved flying over London at as near 25,000 feet as possible. From a close study of fighter affiliation made with No. 111 Squadron, 57 developed the 'Up and Down Formation', where five bombers flew in an asymmetrical V at different heights, which was considered to give 'the maximum flexibility, manoeuvrability and defence'.

The whole squadron was on parade in best blue on 22 September when AOC No. 1 Bomber Group presented them with 'The Cock', and a successful year was rounded off in December when King George VI approved the award of the squadron badge and motto. The design, by Chester Herald, was based on the phoenix motif in use by the squadron for many years and the motto, translated as 'I change the body, not the spirit', recalled the tragic days of that 'Bloody April' in 1917.

January 1937 saw the squadron called upon to provide the initial element of yet another unit in the process of re-formation, No. 108 Squadron. Some weeks later the Record Book shows with some pride that on 9 March, 'Night flying commences. Six pilots went solo immediately', but in April informs that 'No. 226 Squadron, formed largely with 57 personnel, moved out of Upper Heyford'.

The Squadron Drill of low-level bombing by nine aircraft and dive-bombing by three others was a successful feature of Heyford's Air Day that year and, a month later the squadron took part in the mass fly-past, the highlight of Hendon's Coronation Year Display. In the dive-bombing events 57's representative, Sgt H.T. Wood, who had already won both No. 1 Group and Bomber Command competitions, brought further credit to his unit by beating off all comers from other Commands with an error of only 8½ yards and was later presented to the king.

Elsewhere, others were polishing their bombing skills in a different manner. The Spanish Civil War was well into its second year and in a single raid on Guernica the Luftwaffe killed 1,600 inhabitants.

The atmosphere of the September exercise in camp at Henlow was marred by the death of Plt Off M.P.A. Mooney, killed while landing in a field. Tragedy came to the squadron once more a few months later on 23 January 1938, when Aircraftman Goodhand fell from the rear cockpit of a plane during a camera-gun exercise. No similar accident seems to have been recorded by the squadron, even in the wartime days when observer/gunners had performed acrobatics in the shallow-front cockpits of the FE2s, and the irony of the incident was underlined two months later when the squadron took delivery of its first Bristol Blenheim and the association with biplanes and open cockpits came to an end.

The Blenheim Mark I was among the first of the all-metal monoplanes to enter service with the RAF and was crewed by pilot, air bomber and wireless operator/air gunner. With twin 840 h.p. Bristol Mercury radial engines, the Mk I was claimed to be capable of 279 m.p.h. at 15,000 feet and carried a fixed Bren gun firing forward and a Vickers in the dorsal turret. By mid-April, 57 Squadron was completely re-equipped and in May they were chosen to lead the Blenheims taking part in a mass flight to publicize Empire Air Day, following this with a much more sophisticated version of their display on the day itself.

However, aircraft design was leaping ahead, especially where the lessons learned on the

Spanish 'testing ground' had most impact, and within months of coming into service at Upper Heyford the Blenheim was already obsolescent. Dr Roland Winfield,[3] newly appointed Station Medical Officer, enquired of his senior medical orderly, 'What do the crews think of the machines they fly?' 'Flying coffins, sir,' was the reply. 'Very unpredictable, except as coffins.'

Despite the mounting tensions, the usual exercises were held in August 1938, but the Munich crisis brought them to a premature halt. By the end of September all leave had been cancelled and 'peace markings' were removed from the machines, leaving them in drab, camouflage finish, identified only by the squadron code letters EQ, later changed to DX. Night flying continued into the autumn, though one pilot of the era recorded that it was carried out with paraffin flares and 'a very slight idea of the real uses of the Night-Flying Panel'.

The uneasy peace survived the winter and by April 1939 the squadron, now relieved of its task of giving birth to further squadrons, was settled at a 'peacetime establishment' of Wing Commander, 2 Squadron Leaders, 2 Flight Lieutenants and 22 other pilots in the total complement of 227.

As usual, dozens of aerodromes were open for what was to be the last Empire Air Day on 20 May 1939, and a million spectators attended. Among the guests at Heyford were the mayor, town clerk and council of Cheltenham, the squadron having been recently 'adopted' by the town; for some time it was known as 'Cheltenham's Own'. Later in the month the squadron supported the town's National Service Rally by making 'bombing raids' and a mock gas-spraying attack as a thousand volunteers demonstrated their ARP skills.

Bombing exercises at Boscombe Down in August were chiefly remembered by one participant for the filthy weather and the 'hang-up' that resulted in his inadvertently jettisoning a stick of 30 lb HEs on a gipsy camp and a herd of cows, followed, he recorded, 'by a very smart return to Heyford'!

NOTES TO CHAPTER 3

1   Despite its title, ADGB (disbanded in 1936) was primarily a bomber force.

2   HMS *Centurion*, built in 1912, survived to end her days as a blockship, part of the Mulberry harbour at Arromanches, 1944.

3   By the end of the war, Dr Winfield was this country's foremost authority in the field of aviation medicine.

CHAPTER 4

Return to France

Wg Cdr H.M.A. Day AM took command of the squadron on 21 August 1939, and he found morale high. The airmen aircrew did not soon forget their first encounter with this man of skill and enthusiasm. They shuffled to their feet as he arrived for introduction and were somewhat startled as he roared 'Stand up, blast you!' However, they soon came to recognize a born leader and he was popularly known as 'Wings', though his nickname in earlier days, serving in the Middle East, had been 'Happy Day'. (A fellow officer of the time recalls him as 'the pilot I would have flown to Hell and back with,' adding as an aside, 'drunk or sober'.)

In less than a fortnight Wg Cdr Day was to see his unit finalize its preparation for war. General Mobilization was announced and on that fateful Sunday when the 'balloon went up', reservists were arriving at RAF stations in their thousands.

For a short period, 18 and 57 Squadrons were attached to No. 6 (Training) Group but orders came shortly that they were to join HQ, Air Component of the British Expeditionary Force. After a vain, but monumental attempt to drink the considerable wine cellar laid down in the Officers' Mess during their residence, the squadrons were prepared for their return to France.

Sixty-four members of 57 Squadron made the journey to Southampton in an assortment of vehicles – forty-five in all – towing thirteen trailers and comprising such things as radio vans, mobile workshops, field kitchens and tankers for water, fuel and oil. (When the 15 cwt truck carrying 57's share of the remaining wine was hoisted onto the quay at Brest, it was found that the load had evaporated, bottles and all!)

An advance party, also numbering 64, was flown out in Harrow transports, but the main party of 270 officers and men travelled by rail. A three-hour wait for the troop train caused a rush on the Bicester pubs but eventually No. 57 Squadron was on its way back to France; after twenty-three years the wheel had turned full circle.

By 20 September the ground personnel were reassembled at the village of Amy on the borders of Picardy and the Somme. A grass airfield was laid out in meadows still uneven from the days when the Hindenburg Line had stretched across them and by the time the Blenheims flew in on 30 September the village bulged at the seams with the influx of airmen. The squadrons' combined strength numbered almost a thousand. They slept on straw and every barn and byre became a billet, just as they had been so many years before – indeed, German helmets and other relics were still to be found in odd corners of the farms.

For the first three days the rations were provided ready-cooked by the French soldiers guarding the airfield. For breakfast, bread and coffee, for lunch, soup, bread and wine, and similar for supper. However, soon the Record stated, 'British rations have now arrived and the men are happier. They said their complaint was not about the rations, just the cooking.' The Orderly Officer's less formal comment was that the food was 'bloody awful'. So much for cordon bleu.

The aircrews were billeted in the village and the little school served as flight offices and crew-rooms. MT was parked in a farmyard across the road, and petrol and bomb dumps were concealed in the surrounding woods and orchards.

Under the command of AVM C.H.B. Blount, the Air Component represented a gesture of co-operation in the air with the French and consisted of Lysander aircraft for Army Co-operation

The Bristol Blenheim Mk IV, as flown by the squadron in the first year of the Second World War (IWM CH761)

work and tactical reconnaissance, Blenheims for strategic 'recce' and bombing, with Hurricanes and Gladiators for defence. (Fairey Battles were also thrown in to add some offensive weight and were to be punished severely.)

Training flights were soon organized but efficiency was initially handicapped by the non-arrival of supplies and a painful lack of communication. Called one day to Wing HQ in the chateau at Tilleloy, 57's CO was told of the tasks assigned to the squadron. They were to be on standby to provide two aircraft for daylight reconnaissance over the Ruhr area as and when the Army should call upon them. Road and rail movements were to be noted and photographs taken. How little briefing had changed in twenty-odd years. Certainly the aircraft had changed, but how long would these outdated planes stand up to combat with multi-gunned Messerschmitt fighters? Wg Cdr Day was told that the two Blenheims were to fly over Germany by different routes and were to deliver their photographs and reports directly to England. Maj Pattinson had set a precedent in 1917 by leading 57's first operation and Day did not hesitate to lead his squadron into this war. He chose as his aircraft the one usually flown by Sqn Ldr 'Judy' Garland and crewed by the latter's regular crew, Sgt Logan, navigator, and LAC Sid Culver, wireless operator/gunner. For several days they flew practice flights and an advance unit was sent to the French base at Metz to prepare for the arrival of the Blenheims on standby.

By the time specific orders arrived, Day decided that Logan and Culver had been on standby long enough and replaced them. Flg Off Norman of 'B' Flight was to take the other plane, and together they flew to Metz. After an uncomfortable night they prepared for take-off and Day briefed the crews. Norman was to fly the 'Southern Circuit' while Day's own route would take him north, then west towards Dortmund, turning short of Essen and paying particular attention to the Hamm–Hanover–Soest railway.

At 11.30 a.m. on Friday 13 October, Wings lifted Blenheim L1138 from the field at Metz, and with his crew, Sgt Hillier and LAC Moller, headed for the Ruhr. As a former fighter pilot, he knew just how much was being asked of the aircraft and of the men who flew them. Climbing into the forecast scattered cloud, he headed across the Saar and broke the cloud-tops at 20,000 feet. Here, at least, there was some protection. However, fifty miles inside Germany he could see that the 'Met' had got it wrong, for the comforting cloud was gone and below lay Hitler's Reich. Almost immediately flak burst around them, but Day held his course. Too late, they saw the three Me109s sweeping in, line astern, from the port quarter. The cannon-shells hammered along the fuselage as the Blenheim was hauled into a hard vertical turn. As more shells reached their target smoke from the petrol tanks filled the cockpit. Day gave the order to abandon and bailed out. He landed near Langweiler and was quickly made prisoner.[1] Wounded himself, he was stunned to learn that his companions had died, so badly had their parachutes been damaged in the fire.

While the Germans were making their first acquaintance with 'Wings' Day, his No. 2 on the operation, Flg Off Norman, was making his uneventful sortie over the Black Forest, eventually turning northwards. He crossed the North Sea to crash-land in England with petrol tanks dry after a welcome by 'friendly' anti-aircraft fire.

Sqn Ldr A.H. Garland, 'A' Flight Commander, was promoted Acting Wg Cdr on 14 October but two days later he saw the loss of another crew. Flg Off Mike Casey set off on the Southern Circuit and his Blenheim also ended up in flames. Casey and his crew, Sgt Fripp and LAC Nelson, bailed out successfully to join Day 'in the bag'.[2]

On 23 October the squadron moved to Rosières in northern France and the Operations Record Book announced that their duties were to be changed to tactical reconnaissance over the Siegfried Line, their sector extending from Cleve north to Claudeshielde. Perhaps it was thought that this work might be a little more practical for the outclassed Blenheims. Be that as it may, there was virtually no change in the actual operations. On 5 November a Canadian, Plt Off Grant, made a forced landing near Lincoln after venturing deep into Germany, and five aircraft were lost in the first two weeks of the month. Severe icing conditions forced one Blenheim down in Belgium on 16 November and the crew members were interned.

Despite the losses, morale remained high and sometimes youthful exuberance induced pilots to 'beat-up' the airfield – it was considered a poor effort if no one ducked. This practice came to an abrupt end after a tragic accident. One pilot set his plane to cross the field so low that his wing-tip struck a tent pole. Although he managed to haul the machine with its damaged wing to a height sufficient for his crew to escape, he died in his attempt to land.

Early in December Wg Cdr R.H. Haworth-Booth arrived to take command and it was at this time that the squadron was honoured by a royal visit, being among the units inspected by the king during his tour of BEF bases. Through December, bad weather caused flying to be all but abandoned for the month, though Flg Off Nind landed safely with the results of an 'in depth' reconnaissance. Generally there was plenty to be done, for guards had to be mounted constantly on the dispersed sites and dumps. Airmen aircrew were expected to take their share of these duties, as well as being responsible for the daily maintenance of their radios and guns.

The social side of things was not forgotten and the festive season was celebrated with, perhaps, a little more sophistication than 57's first Christmas in 1916. For regular entertainment the 'Liberty Lorry' ran to Meharicourt where the cinema showed English films starring Jessie Matthews, George Formby, the Crazy Gang and the like. Each Thursday bingo was played 'in the hut behind the Canteen', while those lucky enough to see Gracie Fields on stage at Amiens spoke of a truly remarkable performance. However, the entertainments and pleasures may well have been tinged with sadness. By the year's end, almost half the crews who had come over

The No. 57 Squadron badge awarded by King George VI in 1936. Motto – 'I change my body, not my spirit' (Official, via author)

from Upper Heyford had been lost, casualties in what some (safe at home) liked to call 'the phoney war'.

The New Year saw no improvement in the weather and it remained bitterly cold – on several occasions the rum ration froze. By 7 January the airfield lay under deep snow and was almost unserviceable until the end of February, though somehow a few crews contrived to fly the aircraft back to England to exchange them for the faster long-nosed Mark IVs, the process of re-equipping taking nearly three months in all.

The Commanding Officer returned from leave on 2 March but was taken into hospital on 10 of that month so, once again, Sqn Ldr Garland had the acting (and unpaid) extra half-ring on his sleeve. Orders he found it necessary to issue at this time make interesting reading:

Closing time in estaminets and bistros is 21.30 for other ranks, 22.30 for officers. [The peacetime habits of the Regular RAF were still being observed; for example, senior NCOs were not allowed to drink in establishments used by the 'troops'.]

Aircrews are to take compulsory daily runs, unless taking part in organised football or rugby matches.

It has been brought to official notice that Service personnel are attending cock-fighting meetings. [While admitting that such functions were legal in France, it was pointed out that] the principles are not in accordance with British ideas of clean sport and such visits are to be strongly discouraged.

Finally, personnel were reminded that if unexploded shells or bombs were found, the location was to be reported to the Sqn Wt Off. 'The *delivery* of such articles is to cease.'

March saw the presentation of the squadron's first gallantry awards; to Flt Lt G.M. Wyatt a DFC, and to Sgt Thomas and Cpl Culver DFMs. The citation for the latter award records that the recipient was 'the first member to carry out a second reconnaissance over Germany . . . both flights involved fighting in the very cold weather for very long distances. His conduct and ability during these flights had a good effect on the aircraft crews at a time when the Squadron suffered losses.' Frozen cameras and the collapse of observers from lack of oxygen are recorded for several flights during the month, though only three sorties were made over enemy territory. One plane was lost, two of the crew being killed.

Nothing is recorded of the squadron's actions in April, for the Operations Record for that month was lost during the final evacuation to follow, but even during the first week of May they continued 'Flying Practice'.

Suddenly, however, the war took a very different form and on 8 May a 'No. 1 State of Readiness' was ordered and preparations were made for a move. Swiftly the enemy invaded the Low Countries and had broken through French lines at Sedan by 10 May. On the following day another of 57's planes was lost. On 12 May another dropped bombs on Chaulnes, their first offensive action of the war.

Refugees packed the roads and 'fifth column' rumours ran like wildfire, hindering the gathering of accurate information on enemy movements, Despite this, the Blenheims made many bombing and low-level attacks on German tank and troop columns as they advanced, but the situation was rapidly becoming chaotic.

Nor was the bombing one-way traffic; the airfield was subjected to frequent strafing. Two Gladiator fighters were stationed there for defence and as one landed from a sortie it taxied into a starter trolley and the propeller was deformed into a gentle S. At that moment the air-raid warning sounded once more and the pilot turned straight round and took off. On his return he swore that the Gladiator was faster as a result of this harsh modification!

Early on the morning of 17 May it was decided that supporting sections such as the Officers' Mess should begin to pack, but by 10.00 hours orders came through that the whole unit was to move out – and fast. Before they could get under way, fifteen Me109s swept across the field, guns blazing. Surprisingly, only one Blenheim was put out of action.

By next morning the squadron was camped in a field at Poix, with their vehicles concealed in a wood. Even in retreat they hit back as best they could; en route to Poix the Blenheims bombed armoured formations at Le Cateau – ironically, a target in 1917. In the evening six machines took off to attack the enemy once again but on their return, with three of the aircraft badly shot up, they found that orders had arrived in their absence for the unit to strike camp and make for Crécy.

The aircraft were to fly to Abbeville but those damaged in the raid and one other in need of major repair had to be abandoned. Into each fuselage a Very cartridge was fired and they joined the list of 279 aircraft lost to the Air Component alone during this short, sorry campaign.

Through the night the convoy ground its way, arriving at Crécy at 6 a.m. on 19 May. They rested in such shelter as they could find until 17.30 hours, when they were told to move on to Boulogne. Along the way they were under air attack and on arriving at midnight they found the port undergoing constant air raids.

Meanwhile, the surviving Blenheims had been flown across the Channel to Lympne, but for the MT drivers there was more to be suffered for they were told to take their vehicles to Cherbourg. Despite the Luftwaffe's efforts they managed to get there and, eventually, embarked. Between the raids, Wg Cdr Garland got his bedraggled unit aboard the Isle of Man packet *Mona's Queen*. Once under way, a roll-call revealed a total of 3 officers and 298 men, though there was no sign of a Plt Off MacCartney.

By 11.30 hours next morning, they found themselves at Tidworth, guests of a Scottish infantry regiment. One night under canvas and they moved again, to Wyton, where the squadron rapidly re-formed. Immediately they were ordered back into action and a detachment flew down to Hawkinge.

On 23 May Sqn Ldr Foulsham and Plt Off Hutchings took off to make reconnaissance flights. The latter returned with a damaged aircraft and wounded crew, having been attacked by a formation of Me110s. They had, however, shot down one of the enemy on his first 'pass', and his formation leader later, as a result of which Hutchings received an immediate award of the DFC. On a similar 'recce' on 25 May Plt Off Nind's plane was attacked and Sgt Logan received a severe leg wound from the solitary explosive bullet that found its target.

For two weeks the detachment operated from Gatwick Racecourse, being billeted in the grandstand and other buildings, finally returning to Wyton on 11 June. On 23 June the squadron was ordered on detachment to Lossiemouth, Morayshire, where it was to join No. 21 Squadron, on loan to Coastal Command. Bomber Command had put up a spirited, but not altogether successful resistance to the use of Whitley bombers on anti-submarine duties but had to part with a few outdated Blenheims.

Cpl John Holmes joined the squadron at this time; deemed medically unfit for aircrew duties, he dropped a rank from his category as Air Observer with No. 40 Squadron and reverted to his old trade of Metal Rigger. He was put in charge of a small flight and one of their first tasks was to paint the squadron code letters (DX) on newly delivered aircraft. They taught themselves sign-writing but the next requirement was beyond them. They were set to repaint the camouflaged undersides of the Blenheims duck-egg blue to befit them for their maritime role. These chaps knew all about dope-cans and brushes but had never seen a spray-gun, and masking tape was unheard of. They did their best but soon got the sack.

Meanwhile, the detachment in Scotland flew many hours of navigational exercises until, on 9 July, six crews and a similar number from 'Twenty-one' were briefed for an attack on enemy shipping at Stavanger, Norway. They took off at dawn, but the raid, led by Wg Cdr L.C. Bennett, CO of No. 21 Squadron, was a tragic failure.

The aircraft were met by intense flak over the target, followed by a running battle with Messerschmitt Bf109s and 110s. The Blenheim's single Vickers gun being no match for modern multi-gun machines, the one-sided fight continued for some twenty minutes over the sea on the homeward leg. Wg Cdr Bennett's aircraft and four others from his command were lost. The sixth recovered to Lossiemouth, badly damaged. Plt Off R.A. Hopkinson and Sgt F.G. Mills from 57 Squadron failed to return. The surviving crews told of seeing their colleagues falling into the sea, though the last 'Vic' of three, led by 57's 'Freddie' Foulsham, turned right instead of left and escaped unscathed. It might be argued that although little threat was posed by such actions, at least they kept German fighters away from the Battle of Britain in the south.

In mid-August, Cpl Holmes travelled north, just as the squadron moved to a satellite airfield at Bogs o' Mayne. He recalls the accommodation there very well: 'army bell-tents, *c.* 1918, with built-in bunks, eight men to a tent. The cook-house was a field kitchen, *c.* 1896, and we ate in a cleaned-out barn.'

He recalls, too, a weakness in the tail-wheel fitting of the Blenheims. A reinforcement kit was evolved, to be fitted by riveting. This meant that someone had to crawl inside the narrow rear fuselage to hold up the rivets. Only one man on the unit, an ex-jockey, was small enough, and an order was issued that he was not to be posted under any circumstances!

On alternate days for the next ten weeks 57 flew regular anti-shipping sweeps over various areas of the North Sea, sharing the duties with No. 21 Squadron. The purpose of these operations was to prevent enemy capital ships and, if possible, U-boats, from slipping unseen into the Atlantic convoy routes while, at the same time, keeping a watchful eye on unescorted Allied vessels.

Observations were reported directly to Coastal Command and the Admiralty and little detail is recorded in the ORB. For many weeks the entries read simply: 'Six aircraft on shipping sweep', though a plane was lost on one occasion. A little later, Plt Off Taylor and crew shot a Dornier into the sea, whereupon three German planes attacked the airfield. One entry would surely have made a story on its own but states, briefly and mysteriously, 'Barrage balloon captured.' In October we are informed that the Officers' Mess had moved to Blackfriars Hough, Elgin, while the Sergeants' Mess was newly installed in the Oakwood Tearooms.

However, the comforts of the new messing arrangements were not to be enjoyed for long. A memo dated 28 October warned No. 18 Group, Coastal Command, that 57 Squadron was to be withdrawn. The sweep planned for 30 October was cancelled, ostensibly because of bad weather. Two marquees were blown down but before the day was over all 57's aircraft had been flown back to Wyton, the CO making the journey in his Tiger Moth 'hack', presumably with a tail wind. The main parties travelled by rail and though authority was given for the issue of 24-hour ration packs in the form of sandwiches, plus 2s (10p) per man, the CO reported later that notice of the move had been so short that this had not been possible. Once again the poor MT drivers got 'the sticky end', their journey taking four days, and petrol, food and shelter having to be begged on the way.

NOTES TO CHAPTER 4

1   If, so early in the war, the Germans were using that famous phrase 'For you the war is over', in the case of Wg Cdr Day they could not have been more wrong. For 5½ years he continued to fight his war. Escape was his duty and he never forgot it. Leading, inspiring and encouraging others, time and again he got away. Each time he was recaptured, brought back and thrown into the 'cooler'. If the Luftwaffe could not keep him safely, the Wehrmacht must do so. He got out again. Eventually the Gestapo tired of collecting him and put him in the death cells of a concentration camp. When, at last, the chains were removed from his ankles Day started another set of plans and another tunnel. This time he got to Berlin. He escaped nine times in all.

    As the war drew to a close he was taken with a group of other *prominente* prisoners to the southern redoubt. It was his air of authority that persuaded the SS guards against carrying out their orders to 'liquidate' their charges and eventually he was instrumental in bringing about the rescue of the entire party by American infantry. Already the holder of the Albert Medal, (converted later to the George Cross), by late 1945 Wg Cdr Day had been awarded the OBE and DSO for his unique, persistent war. He died in Malta in 1977, aged 79.

2   There was a tragic sequel to the story of Flg Off Michael Casey. He and another pilot from 57 Squadron, Flg Off Anthony Hayter, were among the fifty officers murdered by the Gestapo in the malevolent retribution that followed the 'Great Escape' from Sagan, May 1944.

CHAPTER 5

Joining the Bomber Offensive

As squadron members joined in the service marking Remembrance Day at Wyton in November 1940, many must have looked back over the past year with sadness – so many friends lost, so little achieved. The immediate future for 57 was that they were to join No. 3 Group, Bomber Command, and re-equip with the Vickers Wellington.

They moved to Feltwell on 20 November, the new aircraft arriving later when the dense fog had cleared. Already occupied by No. 75 (New Zealand) Squadron, Feltwell was a well-built pre-war station, situated in a fairly remote corner of south-west Norfolk. No. 57 Squadron also made use of the satellite airfield at Methwold, a few miles to the north. This was used for some operations, bombs being taken there by road, but returning aircraft almost invariably landed at Feltwell.

The Wellington was recognized as an important weapon in Bomber Command's efforts to carry the war into the enemy's camp and was already famous for its ability to stand up to punishment. With an 84 feet wing-span, the 'Wimpy', as it was affectionately known (after Wellington J. Wimpy, a character in the Popeye cartoons), was considerably bigger than anything that 57 had flown before. In consequence the aircrew element of the squadron increased, each crew comprising captain, second pilot, observer (navigator), wireless operator/air gunner and rear gunner. There were few officers on the squadron, most of the crews being senior NCOs.

Frank Beasley, newly back from an engine fitter's conversion course, recalls the aircraft that awaited him: Wellingtons Mk IA and IC fitted with Pegasus XVIII engines, Mk IIIs powered by Hercules IIIs or XIs and – rare birds – two or three Mk II Wimpys equipped with glycol-cooled Merlin Xs. These, he remembers, had no bomb doors, merely a hole big enough to take a 'Cookie', the 4,000 lb high capacity blast bomb.

Cpl Holmes might have been eager to come to grips with yet another new aircraft type but was landed with a different challenge. Given two or three 'erks' and a small room in a hangar, he was told to get his hair cut first, then set up a 'Dinghy Section'. Dinghies had been, in the past, carried in a valise in the fuselage. Perusal of the makers' manual revealed that there was a stowage behind an engine nacelle. A dinghy was removed and taken for examination. It was fitted with a bottle of carbon dioxide and application of an electrical charge had a dramatic effect. The dinghy inflated instantly, pinning two men to the wall of the room and hurling the corporal through the door! Returning a five-man dinghy to a space meant for a smaller version was eventually accomplished but replacements for the eight wooden pegs that held the cover in place were unavailable. New ones were hand-whittled from the cookhouse firewood stocks, hopefully of equal breaking strength.

Another new arrival in late 1940 was Sgt Bob Jefcoate, a wireless operator/air gunner. He had been posted in to join No. 37 Squadron but found that they were moving out, bound for the Middle East, so it was with 57 that he began his first tour. Though his first flying logbook was subsequently lost he kept a diary recording much about his everyday activities as well as his operations.

He records that one of his first duties was to swing (calibrate) the loop aerials on two aircraft. This, along with compass-swinging, was usually carried out at Methwold, where there was less

Wimpy over Feltwell (Anon.)

magnetic interference. The constant attention paid to compass and 'loop' accuracy illustrates how dependant the navigators were on this equipment for they had to rely totally on dead reckoning, aided only by 'star-shots' and fixes from the wireless operator. 'Gee' and the other electronic navigational aids were coming into service, but slowly. Wireless operators still carried out a Daily Inspection (DI) on their sets. They also took part in another exercise, the sending and receiving of spurious messages when no operations were planned, for it was known that the Germans kept a listening watch on RAF radio traffic.

Bad weather dogged the training programme, and poor visibility, both by day and by night, led to many bad landings. On occasion, night-flying was curtailed by the presence of enemy intruders on the circuit. Jefcoate recalls numerous Night Flying Tests (NFTs) followed by briefings for attacks on various French ports. His only successful trips during those early weeks were made crossing the road through deep snow to the 'Sally Ann', a canteen run by the Salvation Army – just a wooden hut, but a haven of comfort where all ranks were made welcome.

However, persistence began to show results and, on 13 January 1941, 57 made their first operational trip with the Wellingtons. It was a 'Freshman' sortie to Boulogne, a town that held bitter memories for many still with the squadron. Freshman operations were, as the name suggests, against targets, often coastal, comparatively easy to find at night.

Two nights later Emden was attacked, a much more ambitious affair; the 4½-hour trip was

Sergeant Bob Jefcoate, Wireless Operator, Feltwell, 1941 (R. Jefcoate)

carried out in intense cold, but without loss, though a 'Bandit' intruder was shot down near the station at about midnight.

A few days later, 'ops' were called off because of fog but an air-raid warning was sounded at 01.30 hours. Despite the snow that fell throughout the following afternoon, the Luftwaffe were not deterred and the alert was sounded three more times. HE and firebombs were dropped but all failed to find a target.

Frank Beasley's memories of these constant raids were that they usually took place around midday, generally just one aircraft being involved. The first warning, 'Yellow', was broadcast over the tannoy PA system, quickly followed by a 'Red' and, invariably, bombs and gunfire. One form of defence employed was the firing of a rocket which carried a wire supported by a small parachute, hopefully into the path of the enemy plane.

Air-raid shelters were situated each side of Flying Control, which stood among a row of hangars. Another hangar beyond these was occupied by a civilian working party employed by Vickers to effect major servicing and repairs. Jefcoate again:

NFT, then Dusseldorf. Most recalled, but not us! Cloud 10/10. Bombed on ETA. Flak and flares. Followed by a fighter. We took a stranger, a Flight Lieutenant, as second pilot. He took over as we flew out over Rotterdam, pulled the wrong balance cock (fuel) and so shut down an engine. We were coned by a mass of searchlights as we turned over the city. Later found he had been very sick back in the aircraft. He went away off the Squadron!

34

The hard work in building up the squadron must have seemed a labour in vain when, late in January, they were ordered to supply ten trained crews to ferry Wellingtons to the Middle East. This assault on unit strength was carried out over a period of some months. Thus, some of the crews detailed to go abroad were still available to take part in a number of raids.

Returning from Lettens on 2 February the aircraft were diverted to Honington; Feltwell had been attacked by Bandits once more though open fields bore the brunt of the bombs. Possibly apocryphal but persistent, another story tells how one night, as the Wimpys arrived home, watchers on the ground stared in amazement as a German plane joined the circuit and landed, only to take off again as the flare-path was extinguished! Feltwell continued its private war and, seen in retrospect, the ORB entries for 27 February show just a glimpse of 'Dad's Army': 'Enemy aircraft attacked the village during the morning . . . Aerodrome Defence Exercise was abandoned half-way, owing to the presence of enemy aircraft in the vicinity.'

Reading through the Operations Record Book (F540) it is apparent that the upkeep of the squadron's 'diary' had been an additional and unwelcome chore placed in the hands of the Squadron Meteorological Officer. An hour-by-hour account of each day's climate preceded, and sometimes, almost replaced, all other entries. Thus, examination can be rather heavy going, two lines of weather reports being followed, almost as an afterthought, by a note on the unit's operations.

The tedium is sometimes relieved, however, by little gems. For example: 'Air Commodore and Mrs . . . entertained to dinner. Fog developed later', or 'Station Commander's sherry party. No operations', while one appropriate 'operational record' reads: 'Flight Lieutenant . . . to hospital, Torquay, for removal of appendix. Night flying cancelled.' Again, 'heavy precipitation' was carefully recorded for 1 March, then: 'Six aircraft to Cologne. Sergeant Emmerson crashed on return.' (Sgt Emmerson's plane, which crash-landed at East Wratham, was a write-off, but the crew escaped, among them, Sgt Sid Culver, never far from the action.)

Bob Jefcoate's notes are more explicit: 'NFT. Briefed for Cologne. Five hour trip. Load: 2 × 500 lbs, 1 × 250, rest canisters. Lord Privy Seal (Mr Attlee), at Feltwell on return – threw an apple-core at him.'

Wg Cdr S.S. Bartram assumed command on 2 March and, though the commitment to supply ferry crews was still unfulfilled, found a squadron 'striving to become a viable unit'. On 3 March, Jefcoate went to Cologne again: 'It was a fair trip; several fighters followed us. 10/10 cloud over there. Landed Mildenhall. Bus back hit fence on the way. Bed 4 a.m.'

Enemy aircraft continued their attacks in March and on 6 seventeen bombs were dropped, one of which hit a hangar and destroyed a Wellington. Twenty-two bombs plastered the airfield next day. (Happily this did not interfere with Pay Parade, though Bob Jefcoate remarked that £3 10s 0d was scarcely a princely sum for a fortnight's work!) In a further raid, three Wimpys were damaged by machine-gun fire, though only to a minor extent.

'A bright, breezy day' was recorded for 10 March. Jefcoate and co. were briefed for Hanover but take-off was delayed by raids on the airfield. Even so, they were over the target by 23.30, ahead of the rest, and home by 03.00 hours. The squadron's first operational casualty with the Wellingtons was suffered on 13 March when one of six planes to raid Hamburg was lost, though Sgt Harvey and his crew survived to be taken prisoner. On the evening of the fourth, three bombs were dropped on the Sergeants' Mess and four on the airfield.

In Berlin lay vast electrical industries and attacks on these, along with ports such as Hamburg, Bremen, Kiel and L'Orient reflected Britain's concern at the mounting cost of the U-boat offensive. On 23 March, 57 made the first of many attacks on the capital. Cologne, Kiel and Gelsenkirchen also featured on the target list.

French ports harbouring invasion barges, such as Ostend and Le Havre, were also attacked, for

*Debrief after Berlin, 12 April 1941. Bob Jefcoate (centre) flew thirty operations with pilot Ron Fryer (chin on hand) and Alex Blakeman, observer (foreground). Only Bob survived (*News Chronicle, *via R. Jefcoate)*

fear of invasion was still very real. Along with the charts of enemy targets, Operational Planning at Group HQ held maps of the beaches and roads of East Anglia so that the bombers could be used against German troops, should they land. When plans for the evacuation of Feltwell were reviewed it was required that transport be available for 27 officers and 366 other ranks.

In April, the ORB noted with pleasure that Flg Off Nind had been landed from a destroyer 'somewhere in England'. (He actually disembarked at Prestwick, Scotland!) Nind had been among the first to leave for ferry duties and among his companions when their Wellington was obliged to ditch some 70 miles off Gibraltar was Sgt Sid Culver DFM, his 'Wop' on many a Blenheim sortie. They lived to fly again and survived the war.

As a boost to public morale, maximum publicity was gained by having the Press in attendance when the crews arrived home from yet another raid on Berlin on 10 April, though two crews failed to return. Jefcoate's crew featured among the photographs but were to be taken off 'ops' and sent on leave with all their kit, parachutes, etc., en route for the Middle East, via Kemble. They hung around for nearly three weeks. Eventually, a rebuilt Wellington was signed as, allegedly, serviceable and they took off from St Eval, fully loaded, for a night trip to Gibraltar. On arrival, a flap refused to lower and they ran on into the harbour. One of the crew was injured though the aircraft was soon beached. Two days later Jefcoate manned the beam guns of a Sunderland and came home to Feltwell via Mountbatten.

On the night of 7 May another enemy bomber swept along the flare-path, dropping ten high explosive bombs and a shower of incendiaries. Happily no one was hurt – it was Feltwell's proud boast that they suffered no casualties from these regular assaults. However, a Wimpy was burnt out and a certain amount of other damage greeted Wg Cdr J.M. Southwell on his arrival to take over the squadron next morning.

Among the first orders he received were for ten aircraft to be prepared and to stand by to seek out the 'pocket battleship' *Bismarck*, believed to be at sea. In the event, they were not sent off, though on 27 May they were despatched on a fruitless search for a Hipper Class destroyer.

Fifty sorties were carried out in May without loss, most of the targets during the spring and early summer continuing the campaign against the U-boat bases and factories. Gradually the squadron gained strength and on 12 June was able to send fourteen Wellingtons to Hamburg, eight of them flying out of Methwold. Sgt Emmerson was in trouble again when his plane's undercarriage collapsed on landing, while Sgt Ward earned an entry in the Record: '. . . bounced on landing. Went round again, landing at Mildenhall in error.' Some bounce! Three nights later a sergeant observer fell from a stationary aircraft and was concussed. Not all the errors and mishaps were on one side, though, for, on 7 June 'Enemy aircraft bombed Methwold and missed.'

However, this was one of Germany's minor failures at the time. Elsewhere, the enemy seemed to be riding on a wave of success and on 22 June Hitler turned his attention and his guns towards Russia.

The squadron's work during June totalled 118 sorties, and 165 tons of bombs were delivered for the loss of two aircraft. A further two were lost on July's 105 sorties against Münster, Essen and Cologne among others. A raid on Bremen failed when the target could not be found, though Sgt Swift and his crew found and destroyed a Ju88 that night. However, tragedy struck nearer home; three complete crews were killed in crashes during the period.

Jefcoate flew to Bremen on 13 June: 'Solid cloud. Shot up badly, down to 50 feet over Duisberg. Lost, compass playing up. Gunners fired at searchlights.' Duisberg was the named target two nights later: 'Two aircraft lost; one crashed at Feltwell. Twenty-two crewmen missing or known dead.' Visits to Mannheim and Kiel completed Bob Jefcoate's tour of 33 ops and he was posted away for a 'rest' as an instructor at an OTU – but that's another story.[1]

When Bomber Command attacked Berlin on 1 August, Sqn Ldr Freeman and crew were 57's only representatives, their Wellington carrying a 4,000 lb 'Cookie'. It was the start of another highly successful month, for only one plane was lost during ninety-six sorties carried out against such objectives as Duisberg, Hanover, Cologne and Mannheim.

On a lighter note, Frank Beasley retains the enduring memory of a morning when the ground staff were paraded in a hangar, then marched to the NAAFI. Here, they were to be subjected to an FFI – 'Free From Infection' – a medical examination to see that no one had contracted a sexually-transmitted disease. (There were other names in those days.) The doors were closed and an SP took up his post to prevent unauthorized entry as the inmates disrobed and formed a queue. However, nobody had remembered to warn the staff and at ten o'clock sharp the shutters over the counters went up and the 'Naffy girls' were ready to serve their 'char and wads'. Chaos reigned as trousers were hastily pulled up from half-mast! Such were the little events that eased the tedium of long hours of hard work.

A Wellington returning from a raid on Frankfurt in the early hours of 3 September crashed at Stapleford, Cambridgeshire and those aboard were killed, including a second wireless operator. When, in 1969, the people of Stapleford were preparing a history of their village to mark the millennium of their church of St Andrew, one of those involved, Mrs Mary Marsden, recalled the search for details of the bomber that had crashed in their midst in 1941: 'It seemed awful to

The tapestry plaque commemorating the crash at Stapleford (Mary Marsden)

me that we could write about the Iceni in AD 16 but had forgotten boys who had died in our village within a few years.' With the help of the Air Historical Branch, MOD, the aircraft was identified as the Wellington of No. 57 Squadron that had crashed there, just 28 miles from Feltwell, as it returned from a raid on Frankfurt on 3 September 1941.

A tapestry plaque bearing the squadron badge and the names of the crew was prepared to display in the church. In 1970 members of the squadron attended the Dedication, which was conducted by the Revd Norman Hennessy, himself a former member of the squadron and an ex-prisoner of war. Mrs Marsden concludes her story:

> The boys are now remembered each Remembrance Sunday. All the names of Stapleford boys lost in the wars are read out and the names of the crew are read too. In addition, poppies are placed on their graves; even if they were forgotten for many years, they will not be forgotten again.

Cologne featured again on September's list but the most remarkable operations of the month were those carried out against Genoa. On three occasions the bombers, fitted with overload tanks, took off in the early evening and returned more than ten hours later, having slogged over the Alps to deliver three bombs apiece – one each of 1,000, 500 and 250 lb. Through the autumn and into another winter the squadron continued its attacks on these targets along with many in the Ruhr – the 'Happy Valley' – including the Hamm railway yards. A Wellington was

Air and ground crew with the 'floppy' 'M-Mother' (F. Beasley)

lost over Hamburg on 10 October and another pilot was killed that night when his plane crashed at Honington.

Crashing on take-off was the sad end for another crew in December but, on 13, luck held for 'R-Robert'. Returning from a raid on Dunkirk docks, three Me110s attacked. When his rear turret was put out of action the gunner moved to the front position, his colleague there having been wounded. Eventually, he too was hit and the front guns rendered useless. By now the sun was rising and the 25-minute action ended in daylight when the enemy withdrew, probably out of ammunition. There was some satisfaction for the battered crew when smoke was seen pouring from one of the Messerschmitts as it headed for home.

Another wartime Christmas was to be celebrated as best could be – for some reason, John Holmes, now a sergeant, shaved off just half of his moustache. For the crews, however, it was still a case of 'press on regardless'. The crew of 'A-Apple' reported being attacked over Düsseldorf on the morning of 28 December by a fighter fitted with a blue searchlight in the nose.

The weather greatly reduced the number of operations through December and January, for that winter saw the worst flying conditions recorded for fifteen years and icing was a constant problem. Even so, the sixty-seven sorties carried out cost but one aircraft to enemy action, though there was another fatal take-off crash early in the New Year.

To add to the general gloom of that wartime winter, the news from the Far East seemed to get worse daily as the Japanese swept all before them and captured Singapore.

Right through February the weather continued to be Germany's best defence from air attack – and, indeed, brought relief to the citizens of Britain's blitzed cities. No. 57 Squadron's sole operation that month was on the 12th when Hitler's *Scharnhorst* and *Gneisenau* made their sudden and seemingly successful dash for home. Six aircraft were despatched to bomb the *Scharnhorst*. Of these, only Sgt Heald in 'K-King' caught a glimpse of the elusive and well-protected target before she vanished again into the swirling snow-clouds. Nevertheless, he dropped his seven bombs and hoped for the best.

Spring drew near and the weather improved. In March the squadron put out seventy-six sorties, including a 'Nickel' raid when leaflets, scornfully called 'bumf', were dropped on Paris. One Wellington was lost over Lübeck on 28 February but when the crew of 'W-William' returned from this raid and claimed to have shot down a fighter, they found they had the Interrogation Officer's prime requirement – witnesses. The gunners of 'N-Nuts' had seen the action and for once it was possible to dispel a little of the doubt from one of these traditionally suspicious individuals. The gunners of 'S-Sugar' claimed to have hit a searchlight-equipped fighter.

The next month started in a most dreadful manner for 57; of a dozen planes sent to bomb Hanau on the very first night, five were lost. Four more failed to return from other operations during April; the total of 121 sorties included two attacks each on Hamburg and Essen.

Wg Cdr Southwell relinquished command on 8 May after exactly a year in office, during which time No. 3 Group recorded: 'Results place this Squadron among the foremost in the Group.' Newly promoted, Wg Cdr Peters-Smith took command of the squadron he had served as 'A' Flight Commander since the arrival of the Wellingtons. Command of 'A' Flight was taken over by Sqn Ldr Laine, fondly known as 'Cowboy Joe'. His favourite aircraft was 'A-Apple' and he was loath to allow others to fly her. Fortunately, no one else wished to, for she was prone to a continuing series of troubles and was 'U/S' much of the time. Laine, however, seemed able to coax her into action. 'M-Mother' was known as another 'maverick', with a history of sagging fabric covering which was never cured.

May proved to be a more fortunate month, only one aircraft being lost. On 29 May Sgt Moore and two of his crew were picked up by the Air-Sea Rescue Service after ditching off the Dutch coast. Cologne was the objective on 30 May when Operation Millennium, the first of the headline-catching 'Thousand Bomber Raids', was launched. All available squadron strength was thrown in and 57 was the strongest with its twenty crews. (Many training units also took part, providing crews of instructors with the more advanced of their pupils so that the magical four figures could be reached.)

An 'advance party' of SNCOs of the USAAF arrived at Methwold for a short spell of 'night-flying experience'. There was no perimeter lighting or control tower, just goose-neck flares and a caravan at the runway's end. They assured their hosts that their squadron could not possibly operate under such primitive conditions. John Holmes comments:

> We did it there for two years and I only recall one crash. An undercarriage leg collapsed and the aircraft ended up on the road, sitting on a 4,000-pounder like a pregnant duck. An army officer arrived to take charge of the situation but left quickly when told that the bomb was very much alive. We had no crane available, so resorted to a set of shear legs. These collapsed with the extra weight, giving the cookie another shaking.

For the next four months the squadron played a constant role in Bomber Command's summer offensive against the Reich, visiting such places as Hamburg, Emden, Duisberg, Mainz, Frankfurt and more, the names reading like a guide to industrial Germany.

At this time, most aircraft carried explosive 'cable-cutters' on their wing leading-edges as protection against barrage balloons. Airframe fitter Ted Vaisey remembers listening with amusement as an engine fitter explained the dangers of these devices to a newcomer. He spoke

Sqn Ldr Laine, 'A' Flight Commander, with his flight and his favourite, if troublesome, 'A-Apple'. He is flanked by Flt Sgt Booth (right) and John Holmes (F. Beasley)

in a broad Yorkshire accent – and lurid detail – of the dire consequences should any part of one's anatomy enter the gap in the device. They were atop a maintenance platform and he gently tapped the wing edge with a screwdriver to emphasize his words.

Suddenly, there was a deafening bang – Yorky had inadvertently done the very thing that he had been warning against! The pair were ashen-faced but unhurt, Yorky still clutching the useless stump that remained of his pride and joy. 'Eh,' he grumbled, 'that were me best bluddy cowling screwdriver an' all!'

That particular day remains in Ted's mind for another reason:

Thrusting my arm into a small inspection hole in the wing to check a fitting, my hand contacted something that was certainly not part of a Wimpy, yet was vaguely familiar. There, tucked neatly away between the geodetics, was a pair of very stylish lady's shoes, slightly dope-spattered but otherwise perfect. It caused me to wonder; such things were rationed and would not have been abandoned lightly. What would the Germans have thought had they found them in aircraft wreckage? [In fact, fabric covering in the factories was generally carried out by women and they were issued with a change of soft shoes to prevent damage to their work.]

On a raid on Osnabrück 'B-Beer' was involved in combat with a fighter fitted with no fewer than four searchlights but managed to escape unscathed. On 25/26 June, returning from Bremen, 'D-Donald', captained by Sgt Croston, drove off a fighter at 03.00 and escaped from two more at 03.20 by diving into cloud and dropping to near sea-level. Fifteen minutes later his

No. 57 Squadron at Feltwell (F. Beasley)

front gunner scored hits on a fighter as it turned to attack another Wellington. The remarkable thing about these encounters was that none of the German planes fired a shot, vindication of the squadron Gunnery Officer's maxim: 'Always fire first as an attacker approaches.' All was not success, however, for seven crews were lost during June.

A week after their other adventures, Croston's crew found further action when, en route for Bremen, they shot a Ju88 into the sea. Before the month was out, Bremen tasted revenge. At 15.30 on 27 July Wg Cdr Peters-Smith took off for a daylight attack and was not heard of again. Another fine officer lost to the Service, sent, one may feel, on a somewhat foolhardy venture.

On 30 July Wg Cdr E.J. Laine assumed command of a squadron recorded at Group as being 'in a high state of operational efficiency'. Be that as it may, the 250 sorties carried out in July and August had cost the squadron dear, for eighteen crews had been lost.

However, respite was at hand. Towards the end of August they learned that they were to change aircraft and Groups once more. It was to Nuremburg on 28 August that No. 57's Wellingtons flew for the last time.

NOTES TO CHAPTER 5

1   Bob Jefcoate leapt out of the frying pan when he arrived at OTU. Considering flying instructing to be dangerous, he volunteered to go overseas. Instead of North Africa he was posted to the Dutch East Indies. One operation ended in another ditching. The Japs arrived and he had to grab a rifle and take part in the general retreat from Sumatra. The survivors fought another rearguard action with Dutch forces before joining two thousand others for ten days of starvation aboard a tramp steamer to Ceylon. Bob completed a tour with Wimpy Ic 'wrecks' of 62 and 215 Squadrons, was then commissioned, and eventually got a staff appointment at Cranwell – that bit went right!

CHAPTER 6

Lancasters and
the Battle of the Ruhr

B omber Command's strategic plans underwent a fundamental change when No. 8 Group, the Pathfinder Force (PFF), was formed on 15 August 1942. No. 5 Group's contribution to PFF, No. 83 Squadron, was the new body's sole Lancaster unit and No. 57 Squadron was ordered to Scampton to begin conversion to Lancasters so as to take their place.

The manning of the unit had to be much increased as each aircrew complement changed to comprise pilot, flight engineer, navigator, air bomber (invariably known as bomb-aimer), wireless operator, mid-upper and rear gunners. Furthermore, the bigger, more complex aircraft with twice as many engines as the old Wimpys, demanded a larger support staff. It was not a shortage of manpower, however, that inhibited the conversion, but of aircraft.

The qualities of the Lancaster had been quickly recognized and the seeds of the legendary fame that now surrounds the aircraft were already being sown. Demands to get the new type into action therefore outstripped production and for their initial training 57 had to make use of a few of the Lancaster's predecessor, the ill-fated Manchester. This type did not entirely deserve its reputation, for it was the unreliability of the engines that brought about much of its failure, while at the same time setting in train the development of its illustrious successor.

Acting Flt Sgt Holmes took an advance party to Scampton to set up 'C' Flight, the Conversion Flight. One Manchester, L7386, had already caught fire and crashed near Scampton, leaving just four to fulfill the task of training the crews. Rarely were more than two serviceable at any one time. John Holmes recalls that the Adjutant insisted that he wore his Observer's brevet and as a consequence he frequently had to act as flight engineer on test flights.

By early September the move was complete and the squadron, now under the command of Wg Cdr F.C. Hopcroft DFC, a pilot of considerable Lancaster experience, soon resumed operations, bombing Wismar on the Baltic coast, and Kiel. Good progress was made and, within six weeks 57 was deemed fit to join No. 5 Group's eight other Lancaster squadrons, together with No. 83 Squadron, specially recalled, in the first mass Lancaster attack.

At Le Creusot lay the giant Schneider arms works where 10,000 workers laboured to turn out vast quantities of tanks, locomotives and guns. Ever since the bomber offensive started, this target had been safely out of reach. It appeared an over-confident gesture to pit the entire Lancaster force into one attack, and in daylight at that. Nevertheless, plans were made for just such a raid.

The route plotted would take the bombers out over the Atlantic, there to turn and fly 330 miles at low level to where the factory and associated installations lay, almost on the Franco–Swiss border. Strip maps were prepared for the round trip of some 1,700 miles and arrangements were made for the bombers to refuel in the south of England to increase the range. Meanwhile, Coastal Command aircraft were sent on special sweeps over the sea to make sure that U-boats 'kept their heads down' and could give no warning to enemy defences.

The raid, carried out on 17 October, was a great success and all but two of the ninety-four Lancasters returned though there were casualties among the crews. None of 57's planes was lost

The squadron's Lancasters at Scampton, 1942 (IWM CH8645)

but they had the misfortune to run into a flock of birds. Plt Off Bowles was cut about the face when the windscreen shattered and one engine overheated as a result of a bird in the radiator. Sgt A.M. Singer was luckier when 'T-Tare' was struck, though his flight engineer, Sgt King, received damage to his eyes. Two other Lancs from the squadron returned early, Sgt P.I. Singer[1] in 'R-Robert' with unserviceable guns and Flt Sgt Danahy in 'K-King', who lost touch with the formation in low cloud near the Scillies.

The squadron received an exceptional honour on 12 November when the king paid a visit. His Majesty spoke informally to the crews and showed great interest in their experiences.

Of greater interest to the enemy would have been the information that the aircraft were equipped with 'Gee', one of the new navigational aids. No doubt they would be able to make their own deductions from wreckage in due course. Meanwhile, conversion training continued, the flying, both by day and night, being fitted in as the airfield was available. It was soon realized that it put unwarranted strain on squadron resources and the work was transferred to the newly formed Heavy Conversion Units.

Having lost his Conversion Flight – and his 'crown' – Sgt Holmes was Duty NCO one night. As he passed by the rear of a Lancaster, engines 'running up', the rear gunner accidentally opened fire, guns at full depression.

He was so scared that he hung on and emptied the whole seven and a half hundred-weight of ammo into the ground ten feet in front of me. . . . I was very short with him when we next met.[2]

The redoubtable Croston, now promoted Flt Sgt, continued his eventful career; returning from Genoa with severe damage, he and his crew abandoned their plane over Surrey and survived. November's targets included Hamburg, Stuttgart and another Italian city, Turin, five aircraft being lost.

Wg Cdr Hopcroft (right) with his navigator beneath Frederick III *(IWM CH8908)*

The waste is sharply illustrated by the short, tragic story of Plt Off Walsh, who joined the squadron at the beginning of November, won an instant DFC, a bar to the decoration a week later and was dead, killed in action before the month was out.

The award of the DFC to Sqn Ldr Long brought further honour to the squadron but crashes marred December's operations. The nine raids carried out during the month cost one aircraft, whereas two crashed on returning from 'ops' and another plunged into the ground following a stall near Woodhall. The weather conformed to its usual pattern and deteriorated during the last few weeks of the year; a number of mining operations and an attack on Turin were spoilt by bad visibility. Three raids were made on this city in a week and the last of these, on 12 December, was carried out in the face of extreme icing conditions.

So the year that had seen the introduction of so many innovations in the bomber war, as well as, proportionately, the heaviest losses, came to a close.

The flying field at Scampton was originally established during the First World War and

HM the King talks to squadrom members. (The aircraft in the background is one of No. 617 Squadron's 'dambusting' B.I. 'Specials'.) (IWM CH9949)

although the accommodation was first-class, there were no concrete runways or hard-standings. Consequently, as the rains set in and continued over Christmas the aerodrome soon became almost unusable. To the unconcealed delight of all, the squadron stood down and over a hundred airmen and airwomen – for by now the WAAF was playing an increasingly important part in the work of all the bomber stations – were able to spend Christmas or the New Year at home.

By their return, little had changed. Water stood in pools and remained for the rest of January, only essential flying being permitted. Even so, the squadron continued to operate. Duisberg, Hamburg and Berlin (twice) were attacked and six aircraft were moved to Fiskerton for a raid on Düsseldorf. The month's tally of seventy-two sorties cost two planes missing and yet another crash when one of the Lancs returning from Berlin collided with high-tension cables.

Flt Sgt Croston was 'Posted out, Tour Expired' on 21 January after almost a year's operational flying on Wellingtons and Lancasters. Who can doubt that the DFM awarded him in March was hard-earned?

Through February the field drained, though slowly, and the danger of the heavily laden bombers becoming bogged down lessened, but only eighty-one sorties were possible, again for the loss of one crew.

An inexplicable incident occurred on the morning of 2 March when one of the squadron's Lancasters, homeward-bound, collided with another before crashing into overhead cables at Riseholme. There were casualties among the crew of the other aircraft, from No. 9 Squadron, but the pilot managed to land with survivors.

The five-month Battle of the Ruhr began on 5 March and 57 were to play their full part in Bomber Command's achievements – and to pay their share of the cost. Even so, new crews were arriving regularly and the squadron's strength grew as never before. It was planned to raise a third flight on 16 March but the plans came to nought. There was a series of explosions on the airfield on 15 March. Three 4,000 lb 'Cookies' blew up, destroying three aircraft and inflicting severe damage on ten others. Peter Grimwood, who began his tour as a sergeant pilot in January of that year and finished it in August as squadron adjutant, recalls the series of events:

We had borrowed several aircraft from other 5 Group squadrons. After the usual Night Flying Test on March 14th the aircraft were bombed up and in line ready for the off when the operation was abandoned at the last minute.

The following morning the aircrew were lined up for the usual Squadron parade, in thick fog. There was a blast from the other side of the field and the hangar windows behind us shook. It was obvious that the aircraft, fully loaded with bombs were 'going up'. We all fell to the ground and I can remember saying to my crew, 'Keep quiet, or the Wingco will have us taxiing them away.' He replied, 'Good idea, Pete. Come on!' Several pilots and flight engineers mounted his car and were deposited at our aircraft. These were in various stages of burning and the .303 ammunition was popping off all round. A fitter had apparently accidently set off a delayed-action photo-flash from an unfamiliar flare-chute on a borrowed aircraft, ran to the nearest slit-trench and got away with it.

Believe me, trying to start the engines of our aircraft in thick fog, just my flight engineer and no trolley-acc [a portable generating set used to boost the aircraft batteries] was a baffling task! Eventually we started two engines and, at full throttle, careered off into the fog across the airfield. After putting as much distance between us and the other aircraft as possible, we eventually stopped and waited for a 'pick-up'. After hours, when the fog had lifted, they found us, not on the airfield but in some adjoining pasture! The aircraft was badly damaged and others were just a scorch-mark on the ground.

As well as this loss of planes, a further reduction in the squadron's strength occurred on 21 March, when five complete crews were posted to a new squadron being formed at Scampton. Sqn Ldr Melvyn Young DFC, chosen to be senior Flt Cdr of the new unit, with Flt Lt Bill Astell DFC as his deputy, was among the captains. Even 57's 'Disciplinary NCO', Flt Sgt 'Chiefy' Powell, was 'stolen', destined to become the right-hand man to his new CO, Wg Cdr Guy Gibson DSO DFC. Well-remembered faces and more and more strange ones continued to arrive, new aircraft were delivered and 57 felt obliged to give all the help they could to the new unit – including the loan of parachutes when they were not actually operating!

Despite these setbacks, the squadron could claim to have carried out more sorties in March than any other in the Group, a total of 102, for the loss, in action, of one aircraft.

Members of 57 were just as curious as anyone else – and not a bit better informed – as to the purpose behind the influx of 'new boys'. While they continued their 'ops', throwing their weight into the Battle of the Ruhr, the 'other lot' seemed to do nothing but lots of low flying, dangerous, exciting stuff that would have put other pilots 'on the carpet'. Even when the new squadron was identified as No. 617, it meant nothing; new squadrons were continually being formed at this time.

Eventually, of course, the world was to learn of the remarkable dam-busting raids and 57 realized what their now-famous neighbours had been about, though they learned with sorrow that their former colleagues, Young, Astell and their crews were among those who would never return. ('Dinghy' Young earned his nickname by ditching on two previous occasions. This time the sea was to become his grave.)

Duties of a lighter nature came 57's way on 3 April when twelve of their Lancasters circled Lincoln while other members of the squadron marched in the city's 'Wings For Victory' parade, a National Savings event. Later in the month, when a similar parade was held at Cheltenham, Sqn Ldr Smith was sent to renew the old ties with the town. A press release issued at the time maintained the anonymity that security demanded, but mentioned that the squadron the town was asked to support had old associations with Cheltenham and had been involved in the bomber offensive, over thirty of its members having been decorated.

Crews being briefed on 20 April were given orders that sounded distinctly 'dicey'. They were to make their way to and from Stettin by crossing Denmark at low level. The intention, no doubt, was to get beneath the enemy radar but, as it turned out, machine-gun fire proved lethal, a bomb-aimer and a flight engineer being killed and two aircraft severely damaged. On landing after a raid on St Brieug the crew of 'H-How' reported that as a Lancaster crossed their path some 50 feet below and slightly ahead, its rear gunner had fired a short burst at them; 'After this unfriendly gesture he disappeared to starboard.'

Spezia was attacked on four occasions during April, in spite of Italian attempts to conceal the city beneath a smokescreen. Such attacks on Italy were, however, subordinate to the onslaught on Germany's manufacturing strength which continued to be the prime objective. Two or three times a week the squadron's Lancasters could be seen taking off into the twilight, turning south to where the three towers of Lincoln Cathedral stood on their lofty island. Airmen looking back as the stream of bombers climbed to converge over the coast may have seen the edifice as some symbol of what the war was about; certainly, for many, the silhouette against the dying sun was their last view of homeland or mother country. The bomber war had many facets, not the least being the contrasts. Half a day was enough to separate the back row of the Savoy cinema in Lincoln from the stink of cordite over the Ruhr.

The month's 155 sorties – again, the most by any No. 5 Group squadron – cost six crews. When the giant Skoda arms works at Pilsen, Czechoslovakia were attacked on 13/14 May, the marking was inaccurate and the results were poor. No. 57 broke another record on 24 May by despatching twenty-four aircraft to Dortmund, believed to be the most ever sent by a four-engined unit. However, two crews failed to return, one on their first operation.

It was a happier occasion on 27 May when the squadron received another visit from the king, this time accompanied by the queen and the two princesses. The royal family showed great interest in the bombers and spoke to all the pilots and crews.

Two nights later, the squadron was into action once more, this time on Wuppertal. The Barmen district of the town suffered 80 per cent devastation but all of 57's seventeen Lancs returned safely. During that month of May, the squadron crews put in a total of 1,229 flying hours, and some training was still being undertaken, for it is recorded that fourteen crews had been 'passed out' for Lancasters.

The weather during mid-summer was poor and many operations were cancelled, including one on Berlin. Of the raids completed one was of great importance to Bomber Command, an attack on the Radiolocation Works ('radiolocation' was an early term for radar) at Friedrichshafen. Seven aircraft from 57 took part, each carrying a 4,000-pounder and seven HE bombs. Each made a successful run over the target before making an uneventful journey across southern Europe and the Mediterranean to land at Maison Blanche in North Africa. (The crews had been suitably 'kitted out' with pith helmets and khaki drills before take-off!) The consequent saving in petrol had enabled the greater bomb load to be carried.

No. 57 were the pioneers of these 'shuttle' raids. In later trips, fresh loads of bombs awaited to be delivered on the return journey (but leaving little room for precious stores of oranges and lemons!).

Two Ju88s combined to attack 'M-Mother' on the night of 14/15 June. The rear gunner was killed as the Lancaster escaped, but generally the gunners could look upon June as a successful month, claiming victory over four Ju88s and an Me109, plus damage to four other enemy aircraft.

The award of a Bar to Sqn Ldr G.W. Curry's DFC rounded off the tally of a dozen DFCs and a similar number of DFMs for the squadron's first eight months of Lancaster operation. However, Bomber Command's losses for the month had been heavy. In just two raids of many, Krefeld on 21/22 and Bochum Gelsenkirchen on 25/26, seventy-four aircraft were lost.

By July the weather had started to improve. On 8 July nineteen planes were sent to Cologne, evidence that the increased squadron size was being maintained. The four-month Battle of the Ruhr ended with 13 July's assault on this huge and well-defended area.

Wg Cdr Hopcroft led a flight of three on another shuttle raid when he attacked Milan on 16 July. Although he was leading the main force attack on this city, his colleagues were to bomb Regia before the three aircraft were reunited in North Africa. The 'Wingco' returned on 21 July but Lt Russell (SAAF) and Flg Off Grimwood stayed until the 24th, bombing Leghorn on their way home.

The rest of the squadron were also in action on the night 24/25 July, a night which turned out to be a milestone in the history of Bomber Command, 'Window' being dropped for the first time. 'Window' was the code-name for the metalized paper strips dropped by the bombers to confuse enemy radar, each strip reflecting an 'echo' in much the same way as an aircraft. The principle had been known for some time but, in fear of putting such a valuable instrument into the hands of the Germans, Bomber Command had not dared use it – and it was for the same reason that the enemy held back from taking advantage of it. Their foreknowledge did nothing to prevent the utter confusion that befell the Hamburg defences that night. Seventeen of 57's crews joined in the raid, which was the first of a short, sharp offensive; by 3 August Bomber Command had dropped 11,000 tons of bombs on the city.

Towards the end of July ten planes were sent on high-level bombing practice and Wg Cdr

Hopcroft reached 'new heights' by hauling his trusty *Frederick III* up to 30,000 feet – no mean feat for a Lancaster. This turned out to be one of his last flights with the squadron, since Wg Cdr Haskell DFC took over on 28 July.

News was received that day that Plt Off Haye was back in England. Reported missing from a raid on 13/14 March, nothing further had been heard until, in due course, the Royal Navy vessel that had rescued him from the sea returned home.

Raids on successive nights, 14 and 15 August, were directed against Milan without loss, though five of the crew of 'D-Dog' lost their lives in a crash-landing on their return from the second. On the night of 17 August, Bomber Command despatched about 600 aircraft against a target the public had not heard of before, Peenemünde. Here was sited a large research establishment where hundreds of scientists and technicians, aided by slave labour, were developing the 'secret weapons' of which Hitler boasted so often. The raid was a great success, indeed, almost a turning point in the air war, for it delayed the advent of the V1 flying bombs and V2 missiles by many months and put a stop to the development of other devices. It was not without cost, however, and among those lost that night was Wg Cdr Haskell, flying only his third operation with the squadron.

NOTES TO CHAPTER 6

1   The Sgts Singer were twins from New Zealand and their careers with No. 57 Squadron ran parallel, each being recommended for a commission during November 1942. They were awarded a DFC apiece later and survived to complete their respective tours and return home.

2   Eventually, Flt Sgt John Holmes BEM took his 'conversion' expertise to No. 1661 HCU, Winthorpe. It may not be inappropriate to record the closing remarks of a memoir he wrote many years later: 'I never experienced boredom; at the beginning of the war, flying was an adventure. I was young and had plenty to do, new things to sample, no real responsibility. Then came the long, slow grind of years as groundcrew, working incredible hours, always short of spares. Bad weather enabled aircrew to "charge their batteries"; it only enabled groundcrew to attempt to make up a little leeway. Even promotion didn't mean any improvement, only more responsibility. And yet, I would do it all again.'

CHAPTER 7

630 Squadron Joins the Battle of Berlin

A daunting task faced the new squadron CO, Wg Cdr H.W.F. Fisher DFC, just days after his arrival on 19 August. Concrete runways were to be laid at Scampton and news of an impending move had just come through. The notice of the move stated that two days were to be allowed for the process of movement and was adamant that 'In no circumstances is the move to be allowed to interfere with the squadron's operational requirements.' Despite this, the instruction concluded by reminding those concerned that the 'customary Parade and Inspection on leaving the old station and again on arrival at the new were to be carried out in accordance with King's Regulations.'

As the Lancasters landed at Scampton from an operation on the morning of 27 August, an advance party moved out, bound for a new airfield at East Kirkby, some 30 miles distant. The mobilization exercises to and from North Coates Fitties a decade before, taking nearly a week in all, paled into insignificance compared with the achievements of the next forty-eight hours as the aircraft and countless tons of equipment were transferred, along with over nine hundred men and women.

On the evening of 30 August fourteen crews took off from their new airfield, bound for Mönchengladbach and all returned safely.

Despite the upheaval, time was found to make due note in the ORB of the award, on 28 August, of the Distinguished Service Order to Wg Cdr Hopcroft for his work in leading the squadron and others of the Group during his recent tour; the citation made special mention of his part in pressing home a low-level attack on electrical installations while leading the Milan raid.

East Kirkby was typical of the bomber fields being built on England's eastern flank at the time. The new occupants must have viewed with dismay the Nissen huts with the little coke stoves for heating and, come winter, would sigh for the comforts of Scampton's pre-war barrack blocks. Contractors were still heavily involved everywhere completing remaining tasks – indeed, the preparations for the first operation were made by candlelight, for the Briefing Room was not yet connected to the mains.

Berlin was the target for East Kirkby's second raid, carried out on 3/4 September, but one of the fourteen crews failed to return. The squadron put on a 'maximum effort' of twenty-one aircraft when a raid was mounted against Hanover on 21 September and all returned safely to base. The enemy had soon discovered that this new airfield was in use, however, and the bombers were joined on the circuit by an intruder, a German night-fighter. Though Flying Control put out a 'Scram' alarm as the runway lights were switched off the warning came too late for the crew of 'S-Sugar'. Only two of the crew managed to bail out after the cannon-shells tore into their plane.

The following evening, 23 September, the crews joined in an attack on Mannheim. All but one of the aircraft came home safely. For Flg Off Joe Hogan, RCAF, and his crew of DX 'G-George' the ORB entries were short and factual: 'Took off, 19.15 hours; not heard of again.' However, the loss of this aircraft and those aboard her led to a sequel many years later. At one

This unique photograph shows German officers supervising the removal of DX 'G-George' from the roof of the Grands Magasins building, rue St Honoré, Paris (Jonathan Falconer)

o'clock in the morning a bomber had been heard flying low over Paris. People woken by the sound of gunfire watched as searchlights and anti-aircraft fire swept the sky. The flak battery positioned at Pré-Saint-Gervais found their target and set it on fire. As it lost height many were of the opinion that the pilot was trying to reach the Seine but the stricken aircraft, a Lancaster, crashed on to the roof of a department store. All the crew were killed and onlookers observed that none had been wearing a parachute, which they believed confirmed their view that an attempt had been made to avoid civilian casualties. The crew now lie in the Municipal Cemetery at Clichy.

After the war, local citizens erected a plaque to mark the spot and honour those aboard, identified as Flg Off Joe Hogan, RCAF, and his crew of 57's 'G-George'. It is affixed to the left wall of the Grands Magasins building, opposite. (Photo taken from the Place Palais Royal.) To mark the fortieth anniversary the Mayor of the Fourth Arrondissement, M. Pierre-Charles Kreig, who, as a boy, had actually seen the crash, presented the current CO, Wg Cdr Alan Bowman MBE, with the city's highest award, the Grande Medaille.

Some time later, the store faced difficulties and was sold. During renovation work the plaque was removed and disappeared for some years but, through the efforts of the Paris branch of the RAF Association, it was eventually restored.

Photographs of the site enabled the position to be located, leading to identification of the hitherto unknown Lancaster in the rare wartime photo on this page.

When another Bandit intruder invaded the circuit on the morning of 27 September, the Scram warning was timely and the bombers were diverted to Waterbeach. They came home later that day but as 'V-Victor' turned towards the runway, onlookers could see that both port engines were feathered and were horrified to see her sink to crash on the hill to the north.

On 8/9 and 18/19 October the squadron made further attacks on Hanover. On the latter raid,

TO THE MEMORY
OF THE CREW OF A BRITISH AIRCRAFT
WHO FELL IN ACTION
FOR THE LIBERATION OF FRANCE
BROUGHT DOWN IN FLAMES ON THE
GRANDS MAGASINS DU LOUVRE
DURING THE NIGHT OF 23RD, SEPTEMBER 1943

JOE DOUGLAS HOGAN
CAN.   OFFICER   PILOT
EDWARD OSCAR BRYANT
R.A.F.   SERGEANT ENGINEER
RAYMOND NORMAN MILLAR
CAN.   OFFICER   NAVIGATOR
JOHN PETER CAMPBELL GORDON
CAN.   SERGEANT AIR BOMBER
CYRIL LESLIE KINGSNORTH
R.A.F. SERGEANT WIRELESS OPERATOR
THOMAS PATRICK CHADWICK
AUS.   SERGEANT AIR GUNNER
WILLIAM HENRY ARNOLD
CAN.   SERGEANT AIR GUNNER

Memorial plaque to the crew of DX-G, affixed to the wall of the Grands Magasins building (F. Beasley)

The Grands Magasins building showing the flat roof. On the left is the front of the Palais Royal (F. Beasley)

Outward bound (D. Brown)

Sgt Arthur Cowham, rear gunner of 'Y-Yoke' was wounded in a sudden fighter attack as the aircraft left the target area. The plane was struck by a hail of bullets which caused much damage; Sgt Cowham was hit in the face and suffered severe facial injuries and the loss of an eye. His turret was virtually wrecked but he fought on and helped to drive off the enemy. Throughout the long journey home, despite intense pain and loss of blood, he twice directed his pilot to outmanoeuvre further fighter attacks. (A crew-mate recalls that the gunner was singing between whiles to stay alert!) His citation for an instant award of the Conspicuous Gallantry Medal (Flying) – the NCO's DSO – concludes: 'On this, his first sortie, Sergeant Cowham displayed courage, fortitude and devotion to duty in keeping with the best traditions of the Royal Air Force.'

Constant training was a way of life and there was a flow of 'bods' to and from courses – various officers to the Bombing Development Unit, flight engineers to A.V. Roe Ltd, fitters to Dowty Hydraulics, drivers to Coles Cranes, etc. Almost every day new crews arrived from the HCUs and the newly instituted Lancaster Finishing School. So too did a smaller number of crews, well into their first tour. This influx was far in excess of what officialdom liked to call 'wastage' and the result was the birth of a new squadron. On 15 November the whole of 'B' Flight, commanded by Sqn Ldr M. Crocker DFC (USA), became No. 630 Squadron.

Established at sixteen Lancasters, plus four reserves, 630 had a full complement of aircrew from

Eggs were rationed and the 'flying egg' was a perk much treasured by aircrew (IWM CH12872)

the outset and wasted no time in going to war. The Battle of Berlin was now getting under way and within three days Sqn Ldr Crocker led the new squadron, their Lancasters coded 'LE', on its first operation as it joined the campaign – and their first five sorties were against 'The Big City'.

One of 57's aircraft crashed on take-off that night and another failed to return; they lost two more on the fifth successive raid on the capital on the night of 2/3 December. 'N-Nan' was missing when the rest returned on the morning of 17 December and a Lanc of No. 106 Squadron reported a ditched aircraft. HM Minesweeper *Typhoon* went to the scene to find that the report was accurate, but only the wireless operator survived.

When Flt Lt Cheetham took over as No. 630 Squadron adjutant he met with countless difficulties, all well recorded – in manuscript. The squadron offices had no electric light and could not be 'blacked-out' either. After five days, having borrowed some folding tables and chairs, he got some inexperienced clerical staff and, later, a typewriter. It was later still that a Waaf able to use it came to his assistance. The 'Adj' recorded that the living quarters had no floor covering and toilet blocks were just as the builders had left them – the occupants of the offices were disgruntled to find the nearest latrines were 200 yards away (winter was setting in!). Other problems included the fact that the squadron's forty officers shared but one batman instead of the established ten! The nominal roll at this time showed a total of seventy-eight (NCO) aircrew, and, he says, 'the spirit was cheerful'.

The third raid on Berlin was carried out in severe icing conditions and two of 630's aircraft were lost. On the next raid, 57 lost a crew while Plt Off Edwards of 630 could not identify the runway at Holme and crash-landed there.

Attacks on other German cities continued. Raids on Leipzig and Düsseldorf intervened but Berlin was still the main target and the expensive one, for a crew was lost to 57 on both of the further visits in December. Returning in the early hours of 4 December, 630's JB561 was involved in a series of combats between Brandenburg and Leipzig. Flt Sgt White flew his aircraft home despite extensive damage – starboard inner engine dead, intercom U/S and, apparently, the rear turret, too. He put the plane down safely though both tyres were punctured. Only then was it found that the rear gunner had been killed. The mid-upper gunner survived and laid claim to an Me210 shot down. Flt Sgt White was awarded an immediate DFM.

Cheetham made a careful note on the morning of 11 December: 'A very fine spirit was shown by two humble ACH/GDs who, having worked all day, worked continuously until 08.30 hours in order to give extra cleaning to the Squadron offices.' The reason for his grateful 'mention in despatches' was clear when AOC 5 Group, AVM The Hon. Ralph Cochrane CBE AFC, arrived and stayed for lunch.

On 13 December Wg Cdr A.D. Rollinson DFC assumed command of No. 630 Squadron and was soon in action, flying as second pilot within three days of arrival.

By this time, the two hundred or so inhabitants of East Kirkby were outnumbered ten to one by the Service personnel now living in the domestic sites that surrounded their village. The airmen and women soon settled in and tried to make themselves at home. On 21 December the ground crew kicked off the festive season by throwing a party for the local children. Each received a gift, the results of a toy-making competition held earlier. However, the posh event that evening was a house-warming, the first party in the new Officers' Mess, AOC Group arriving once more to be guest of honour.

Still ops continued, even to the loss of a crew on Christmas Eve. Flying ceased for the day when the luckier crews landed and the old traditions were observed, the officers serving dinner to other ranks and entertaining the members of the Sergeants' Mess in the evening while the rest of the camp enjoyed a cabaret and dance in one of the dining halls.

The adjutant of 630 commented that progress on the 'admin' side had been slow during the month. No stationery had yet been received and he had reached the limit as far as borrowing was concerned. The forty-eight officers now had no batman at all, but they had lino on the floors at last.

Though the weather was bad, time off was limited; operations continued and on the evening of New Year's Day it was Berlin once again – the squadrons lost a crew each that night – and for the rest of January 1944, come snow, fog or frost, this and other targets in the Reich received attention.

No. 57 Squadron was to lose a further five aircraft during the month. Flg Off Castagnola and his crew were 'blooded' in a series of attacks against Berlin when they joined 57 to start what turned out to be a successful tour, completed with No. 617 Squadron in No. 5 Group's own Pathfinder Force. Les Barnes and his crew flew with 630 and their first four operations were to the German capital.

The first of these was a bit hairy; we were attacked over Magdeburg on the way home. 'Jerry' made a couple of passes, my gunners returned his fire and he broke away. My rear gunner claimed a hit as smoke was seen coming from the fighter.

In the morning, the crew went out to assess the damage to their plane and arrived in time to see an unexploded cannon-shell being removed from a petrol tank.

At the beginning of January 1944, the H2S radar that equipped the Lancasters was modified. Normally, the scanner, fitted in the bulbous projection under the fuselage, reflected a 'picture'

They also served . . . LACW Lily Corrigan (left) and ACW Vicky Leonard, Sergeants' Mess, East Kirkby

of coastal outlines and built-up areas. Now, an addition known as 'Fishpond' made use of a portion of the 'cone' swept by the scanner to search for fighters in the bomber's blind spot underneath. During January the crews were tasked with evaluating the new device. Keeping an eye on the little screen was an extra job for the wireless operators and they soon became skilled in the interpretation of the images on the screen. Another regular 'fit' was 'Mandrel', a device designed to interfere with the enemy airborne communications.

At about this time Sqn Ldr J. Vivian DFC was posted out to become Group Navigation Leader. His tour with 57 had been unusual in that, as a navigator he had served both as flight commander and aircraft captain; his departure was marked with the award of the DSO. His pilot on many occasions had been Plt Off J. Joslin, who now received an immediate DFC. This young man had joined the squadron in May 1943 when just twenty years old. His tour had been beset by combinations of all possible difficulties – technical failures, icing, other adverse weather conditions and so on – and these were remarked upon in the citation for his award. In his eight months with 57 his career had followed the pattern of so many, for he had married, been commissioned and now decorated. However, as so often, the pattern continued on its merciless way and John Basil Joslin was killed in a flying accident at Swinderby later in the year.

Other awards at this time were of a Bar to Malcolm Crocker's DFC – quite unique in that he won the DFC with both 57 and 630 – and an immediate DFC to 57's Flg Off Erik Neils

A timely warning (by 'Raff' [Bill Hooper] and Anthony Armstrong) displayed in the adjutant's office

Westergaard. He was one of the very few Danes to fly with Bomber Command; sadly, he did not survive to see his country liberated.

No. 630 maintained a clean sheet throughout January until the night of the 28th when they received a bitter blow. Two of their aircraft failed to return, one of them flown by Wg Cdr Rollinson. Wg Cdr W.I. Deas DFC took over the command on 1 February.

'A Bomber's Moon' had denoted a full moon in the first years of the war, but now that German fighter controllers were able to bring their aircraft within 100 metres of their quarry, darkness was the best protection. The moon period in early February 1944 brought some relaxation but the squadron commanders implemented 'special training'. Crews were deposited around the countryside on escape exercises. Lectures were arranged on all manner of subjects relevant to the aircrews' duties, fuel economy and engine handling being emphasized for the pilots and flight engineers. No. 57 Squadron's ORB notes that the latter were to spend some time in the hangars helping with servicing. Sgt Beasley, NCO i/c No. 2 Hangar, makes a comment on this: 'Never saw anything of 'em!'

It was a bitter winter and many, speaking of the times, still recall the wind that cut across the fields 'straight from Siberia'. To add to the hardships, hot, and sometimes even cold, water was in short supply – a WAAF officer remembers having tea made from melted snow.

There was little respite for the ground crews out on 'the flights', whatever the weather. A stand-down gave them no rest, merely a chance to catch up with the work. Roy 'Lofty' Jones was an armourer and recalls the terribly cold mornings.

To the left, No. 57 Squadron Headquarters at East Kirkby. The frames on the right are stands for working on aircraft engines (L. Wakerell)

Sometimes the guns were so cold they stuck to your hands. There were mornings when your bike-chain was frozen up. I believe it was a cheeky, cheerful Londoner, Joe Craddock, who devised a remedy by peeing on it! It was a sight to behold: a line of propped-up bikes, a line of airmen and a lot of steam! They were a great crowd, both at work and on a rare night off when we let our hair down in the local pub or in Boston.

Our sergeant, 'Jock' Webster, had the knack of being able to 'win' whatever we needed, whether from Stores or Cookhouse – we always seemed to be hungry.

As the moon waned, No. 5 Group returned to playing its part in the Main Force attacks on such places as Stettin, Magdeburg, Leipzig, Stuttgart and, again and again, Berlin. No. 630 could claim to be the strongest squadron in action on 15 February, providing twenty-one of the forty that left East Kirkby that night. All returned though one crashed on landing.

The one exercise that could not be practised during training was to take off with a full load of bombs. A runway of some 2,000 yards was scarcely enough for a Lancaster weighing close on 30 tons; there was no room for error. When 630's Flg Off E.J. Murray, RAAF, bound for Stuttgart on his first sortie, was almost clear of the runway, the aircraft veered to one side. It careered across the East Kirkby–Spilsby road (A155), the undercarriage collapsed, and the entire bomb load exploded. Debris was scattered far and wide but, almost unbelievably, the rear turret was found in a ditch with the gunner inside virtually unscathed, the sole survivor.

Les Barnes also had reasons to remember that night for his aircraft was hit by cannon-shells from below – a typical *Schrägemusik* attack by a fighter with upward-firing cannon. The turrets were put

'Home', a typical 'bed-space', though NCO aircrew at East Kirkby were usually accommodated in the steel Nissen huts (L. Wakerell)

out of action and he dived from 12,000 feet to escape, unaware that the plane was on fire and a sitting duck. When the starboard engines were hit he ordered the crew to bail out, then left his seat and dived for the lower escape hatch. Somehow he got through and landed safely. His luck continued for he met up with members of the French Resistance and began a long journey home.

No. 57 was called on to support the first wave of Pathfinders when Stuttgart was bombed again on 26/27 February, the marking being recorded as 'very accurate'. Stuttgart was to feature twice more in March, as was Frankfurt. No. 57 Squadron maintained a clean sheet for these raids but 630 was punished, losing four aircraft.

The first two months of 1944 had cost the station fifteen aircraft, most of them lost on the Berlin offensive. The last raid of that series took place on 24/25 March[1] and brought Bomber Command its heaviest losses to date, seventy-three bombers. It was a sad night for East Kirkby, for 57 and 630 lost two and three crews respectively. Tony Leyva was navigator of one of these latter and for some reason had doubted the efficiency of his parachute before take-off. Returning it to the Parachute Section, he explained his worry to the staff. They pulled the rip-cord and it worked perfectly. Later, the plane was subject to a violent cannon-shell attack and dived out of control. Leyva was thrown from his seat and out of the front hatch, already open. At first, his 'chute failed to open. He tore at the pack in desperation, the silk flashed before his face and he was left hanging by only one hook. He was swiftly taken prisoner and in the morning taken to view the half-burnt remains of the Lancaster. His friends had all died.

This was the sixteenth Berlin operation the squadrons had shared since 18 November at a

A long night for the Duty Crew (IWM CH12871)

total cost of thirty-four aircraft. In the course of that last raid, the wireless operator of 57's 'R-Robert' spotted 'blips' on his 'Fishpond' screen, indicating a fighter closing in on the slower image of a bomber. He directed his pilot, Plt Off R.A.W. Beaumont, so that they lost height and closed until the mid-upper gunner, Sgt Allen Hudson spotted an Me109 attacking a Lancaster, which was diving to starboard. The enemy broke away and turned towards 'Robert'. The W/Op then directed his pilot and gunners to such good effect that they shot the Messerschmitt down.

As has been seen, bomber losses had increased throughout the winter but the worst was yet to come. On 30 March Main Force set off for Nuremburg, thirty-four Lancasters from East Kirkby among them. For the bomber crews nothing went right that night. The overcast weather that had been forecast cleared suddenly and the new moon showed up their condensation trails; a change of wind brought the first wave of aircraft over the target late and the second too soon. Even mistakes by the enemy controllers turned to their own advantage. Of nearly eight hundred bombers involved, ninety-four were lost and a further dozen crashed on return.

No. 57 Squadron was more fortunate than most, losing but one plane of the eighteen despatched and three crewmen of that plane survived, though 630 lost three of their sixteen crews. On the credit side, 'C-Charlie' was lucky to escape. The rear guns were frozen up but a burst from the mid-upper caused an Me210 to retreat. Castagnola's gunners told of the Ju88 they had shot down and another damaged. Bomber Command produced statistical data: 'An unacceptable 11.8 per cent loss rate.' The survivors simply saw empty chairs in the messes; seven hundred aircrew would not be coming home.

Aside from the crippling losses, the Nuremburg raid was an abysmal failure but this was only one of the reasons for the strategic changes that followed. The plans to put the combined bomber force

No. 630's 'D-Dog' climbing hard (IWM CH12970)

under central command so that they could play an invaluable role in the long-awaited invasion of Europe had been made at the Casablanca Conference, and this new phase was soon to begin.

April's first operation was to lay mines off Danzig. The next, an attack on the airfield at Toulouse, was led by Wg Cdr Fisher. This was one of his last with the squadron, his place being taken by Wg Cdr H.Y. Humphreys DFC on 15 April. The new CO's motto must have been 'start as you mean to go on'. On arrival at HQ one morning he was not best pleased at the sight of his crews in the pose they were inclined to adopt when waiting for something to happen: one hand in a trouser pocket and a fag between their lips. All of a sudden they found themselves formed up in threes – officers as well – and sent off to march around the peri-track to the runway end, then down to the next intersection before returning to base.

Marching along the main runway they presented an opportunity too good to miss for a 630 crew on an air-test. As the Lancaster thundered towards them at zero feet the parade scattered! However, the sight was too much for Flying Control and as the chastened 57 crews recovered with their NAAFI tea they were more than happy to see seven lonely figures retracing their route. They, however, had to march in the opposite direction, which meant that they finished their march right past 57 HQ, where they received loud applause!

The change in the variety of targets soon became evident. The next four targets were all on railway yards, first at Tours, then at Aachen. Juvisy and La Chappelle, on the outskirts of Paris, called for great care in both marking and bombing. Both operations made use of the various marking methods being developed by No. 5 Group and were the most successful raids of their kind

Railway yards at Juvisy-sur-Orge before the raid of 18/19 April 1944 (Author)

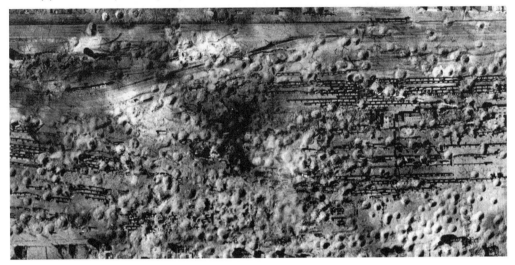

. . . and after (Author)

to date. In each case the bombing was well concentrated and avoided the surrounding residential districts. However, the success was not without cost for 57 Squadron lost an aircraft on the Juvisy raid. All on board died, including a second pilot, when it crashed at Whittlesey, so near to home. A further blow came when 'A' Flt Cdr, Sqn Ldr P.M. Wigg, failed to return from La Chappelle.

Despite the change of tactics that introduced the 'transportation plan' targets in support of invasion schemes, Bomber Command did not lose sight of the main objective, the Third Reich. After a raid on Brunswick two more were 'laid on' using the Lancaster's maximum fuel load of 2,154 gallons before the shortening nights made such ventures impractical. Each was routed in a roundabout manner and after an eleven-hour slog to Munich and back experienced crews reported it as 'the best concentration of attack' they had seen. All but one returned safely, though tragedy was but narrowly missed as the planes took off. The port inner engine of one of 630's bombers caught fire on take-off and it was unable to gain height. The pilot made a tight circuit and, as the port outer also caught fire, made 'a fine crash-landing on the edge of the field'. The fires were swiftly tackled by the fire party as the crew were rescued by none other

'Blue' Rackley, RAAF (fourth left), and crew enjoying a last smoke before taking part in the Juvisy raid (IWM CH12774)

Richard North of the BBC interviews the crew of LE 'S-Sugar' after the raid (IWM CH12778)

Ground crew with Lancaster ND471, 1944 (J. Lett)

than the Station Commander, Gp Capt R.T. Taafe, and the Station Medical Officer, the only casualty being the flight engineer with a broken ankle.

The one aircraft that failed to return straight away from that raid was 'G-George'. An engine caught fire and the pilot, Plt Off L.M. Rackley, RAAF, decided to head for Switzerland before ordering the crew to abandon. Insufficient power to climb over the Alps forced him to change his mind and head for Corsica, by now back in French hands. Landing at Borgo, two more engines cut and in the heavy landing the tail swung and collided with another aircraft, killing the rear gunner. The record was less than sympathetic, making the comment that he should not have been in the turret in an emergency.

The story of the second raid, aimed at Schweinfurt, was very different. The bombers arrived over the target late because of unexpectedly strong winds and the enemy soon got his fighters into the 'stream'. Of the 226 bombers involved that night 23 were lost, among them, one from 630 and two from 57, including that flown by Sqn Ldr M.I. Boyle, 'B' Flight Commander. Two others of the squadron's Lancasters limped across the Channel to land at Tangmere. An immediate DFM was awarded to Sgt Ronald Chandler, the nineteen-year-old rear gunner of 'J-Jig', who had driven off a Ju88, despite horrific cannon-shell wounds that were to cost him a leg. The captain, Plt Off Edgar Nicklin, RNZAF, displayed great skill in landing his crippled aircraft, as did Flg Off Beaumont who followed shortly after in 'R-Robert'. They, too, had been savagely attacked by a Junkers, resulting in the death of the rear gunner and severe wounds to the mid-upper gunner, Sgt Allen Hudson.

Refuelling 'N-Nan'. Hagnaby Grange farmhouse is in the background (IWM CH12868)

Plt Off E. Nicklin, RNZAF (2nd right), and his crew before the Schweinfurt raid, 18/19 June. Lancaster DX-J, LL939, was severely damaged on her second operation (Author)

All the crews taking part in April's last operation, on the Aulna airfield at Clermont Ferrand, returned safely but the month's work had cost East Kirkby eleven crews. Nevertheless, it was recorded that it had been 630's best month, 588 tons of bombs having been dropped in a total of 136 sorties 'and morale and squadron spirits were high'.

Some 15–20,000 troops of the 21st Panzer Division were stationed at Mailly-le-Camp on the outskirts of Paris, making an obvious pre-invasion target. Nos 1 and 5 Groups mounted a most successful attack on 3/4 May, but at a cost, for 42 of the 338 aircraft involved were lost. Successive attacks were made on the airfield at Tours and another rear gunner of 57 was wounded. His pilot, Flg Off Ron Walker, somehow nursed the plane back to a landing at Tarrant Rushton, even avoiding further attacks, though the control column had to be tied forward and the port outer engine had been feathered, rendering the rear turret and the 'Gee' navigation aid ineffective.

An attack on the railway yards at Amiens was a failure because of the weather and the crews had to make a detour out to the jettison area in the North Sea to reduce the aircraft to a safe landing weight. Two nights later, on 21 May, they were over the North Sea again, this time to overfly Denmark en route to Stettin and Duisburg, though most of the aircraft also carried sea mines. Again there was activity from the fighter airfields in north Germany resulting in the loss of one of 630's bombers on the Main Force attack and one from each unit engaged in mine-laying.

During a night flying test on 23 May, prior to a raid on Brunswick, one of 57's Lancasters was involved in a collision with another from No. 83 Squadron. Though the East Kirkby pilot managed to recover to base, the other crew perished as their aircraft plunged to the ground at nearby Revesby.

The 'truant' Lancaster,'Conquering Cleo' 'stolen' by 'Freddie' Watts (centre front) and crew (D. Cooper)

A 'Cookie' for a cushion (E. Watson)

Plt Off F.N. Henley (right), and the crew of the replacement DX-J, NE127. Shot down on 23/24 May, only the gunners, Paul Dalseg and Norman Wharf (1st and 2nd left), survived (J. Mulder)

The Watch Tower – 'Flying Control'. Call-sign 'Silksheen' (IWM CH18718)

The crews of No. 57 Squadron in April 1944. Wg Cdr H.W.F. Fisher DFC is seated between Sqn Ldr Wigg DFC, 'A' Flt Cdr (left) and Sqn Ldr Boyle DFC, 'B' Flt Cdr (Official, via author)

That night, the East Kirkby bomb-bays were loaded with the fearsome 'J' Type incendiary bomb, a 30 lb phosphorus-filled weapon, but the raid was a failure owing to unexpected dense cloud. Nevertheless, it cost 57 three crews. One of these, 'J-Jig', NE127, was shot down by a fighter based at Leeuwarden airfield and crashed at 23.45 hours near the Dutch village of Dorkwerd, to the west of Groningen. Only the mid-upper gunner, Paul Dalseg, RCAF, managed to bale out before the plane exploded in mid-air. By some miracle his colleague, Sgt Norman Wharf, also a Canadian, survived when his turret landed in a deep ditch. Both were quickly captured, but Plt Off F.N. Henley and the rest of his crew perished.

Among the witnesses that night was a thirteen-year-old schoolboy, Auke Noordhof. Deeply impressed by the spectacle, he promised himself that, when peace came, he would do all he could to identify the aircraft and its crew. It took him many years to complete his task but eventually he made contact with the two survivors in Canada and with relatives of those whom he felt had given their lives for the people of Holland. In 1990 a memorial stone was unveiled by the five graves. His friend, Jan Mulder, who helped in the quest, records that 'his efforts were typical of the attitude of the Dutch population, who, after more than half a century are still deeply grateful for the sacrifices that our Allied friends paid for our freedom'.

'A particularly good concentration' was how 57's ORB noted a raid on the Ford and General Motors works at Antwerp on 24/25 May. A couple of nights later, the squadrons joined in an attack which was plainly connected with invasion plans. On the cliffs above St Valéry-en-Caux were six heavy guns, facing the sea. Despite a daylight raid by the USAAF and further attacks by Bomber Command, these weapons survived until that night, when No. 5 Group had their turn. In just twenty minutes, five of the guns were destroyed and the sixth rendered useless with the obliteration of the control gear.

In the period running up to D-Day, the crews were issued with .38 Smith & Wesson revolvers as an escape aid if shot down behind enemy lines. For the few days that the novelty lasted devotees of cowboy heroes amused themselves practising a 'fast draw'! Nevertheless, it had a somewhat sobering effect, seemingly bringing another facet of the war closer.

As the days lengthened some of the crews that had survived the severe fighting of the winter were posted out 'Tour Expired'; for the rest, morale was recorded as high. Until, that is, Command decided to 'move the goalposts'. A rule was introduced whereby all operations to northern Europe were to count as one third of an op. The rule was retrospective and those whose logbooks contained a dozen of the red-ink entries blanched as their 'score' was halved

Sgt R.A.W. Beaumont and crew of Lancaster DX-R (A. Hudson)

overnight, while, for newcomers, the prospect of a ninety-op tour looked bleak indeed. To the relief of all, the rule was rescinded after a week or two and the situation restored. All completed ops were to count in full though tour duration was extended from thirty ops to thirty-five.

The code-name for mine-laying operations was 'Gardening', mines were 'vegetables' and the various target areas had horticultural names. At the end of May, 'V Group News', a wall-newspaper, reported one such sortie: 'A long, low-level flight in near daylight conditions by four aircraft of 57 Squadron is worthy of note.' They took off at 23.40 hours, Double Summer Time, and barely dusk. Their route took them towards the 'Midnight Sun', around the tip of Denmark and down the Skagerrak to plant their vegetables in Kiel Bay. The whole operation was flown at only a few hundred feet and proved quite uneventful, though the display of neon signs along the waterfront of neutral Gothenburg was a spectacle for the crews, used only to flying in black-out conditions.

In 260 sorties carried out in May, nine Lancasters had been lost. Through the month there had been continuing changes of targets as the power and adaptability of the bomber forces were increasingly used in a tactical role. The squadrons operated three times in the first four nights of June, bombing Saumur railway tunnel, a radio station at Ferme d'Urville and gun emplacements at Maisy, typical of the mix of enemy communications and defence installations being attacked in the softening-up period prior to the opening of the Second Front.

NOTE TO CHAPTER 7

1   It so happened that, seated among the Berliners in an air-raid shelter that night, was a well-disguised 'Wings' Day, making yet another attempt at a 'home run'. (See Chapter 4, note 1.)

CHAPTER 8

D-Day and Beyond

The Second Front was on everyone's lips and the build-up of the forces and equipment was plain to see – even the main runway of No. 5 Lancaster Finishing School at Syerston was bordered by rows of Horsa troop-carrying gliders – but the secret of D-Day was well kept.

When the crews assembled for Briefing on the evening of 5 June they were told no more than they needed to know to enable them to bomb heavy guns on a hilltop at La Pernelle on the Cherbourg peninsula. To add to the enemy's confusion, Bomber Command's attacks on such defences were spread along the French coast, the 1,136 aircraft involved dropping 5,315 tons of bombs.

The curious pattern of the tape-marked route raised eyebrows and the over-emphasis on the need for radio silence seemed to indicate that 'something was up'. The route to and from their target took the bombers well clear of the vast fleet of ships and aircraft transporting the troops to Normandy. For the bomber crews, the night was fairly quiet.

Nevertheless, there was excitement enough when the crews landed and heard German radio confirm that 'small forces had landed and were being repulsed'. No. 630 Squadron's ORB recorded satisfaction: 'In the morning, we could see the part we had played.' This particular raid was not, apparently, a complete success, for some guns continued to fire upon the American forces landing on Juno Beach until they were captured some days later.

The crews had little sleep, for the NFT was 'laid on' early, though, in the event, it was past midnight when they took off again, this time to bomb bridges over the Orne at Caen. These were in the path of enemy armour heading for the slender British foothold. Nor was this raid a great success for it was difficult to identify the targets. An aircraft was lost to 630 and 'O-Oboe' was fortunate to survive when raked by fire from a Ju88. The pilot, Ron Walker, who had been awarded an 'immediate' DFC for his efforts returning from Tours some weeks earlier, corkscrewed[1] to safety but the mid-upper gunner, Flg Off Tom Quayle, was found to be dead immediately after the action. The aircraft was badly damaged but reached base, only to have a tyre burst on touch-down.

The squadrons were operating four times a week during this period and the men and women supporting them were particularly hard pressed. For them, there was little time for relaxation – all ground-crew leave had been suspended for four months.

LAC Denis Howell was an electrician working out on the dispersals and well remembers the daily grind:

Like everyone in uniform we worked a seven-day week. The only time we had off was after our turn on 'Duty Crew' on ops nights. We would usually arrive at the flight hut at 8.00 am. There, the corporal would allocate the aircraft for DI and hand out the list of snags reported by the aircrew. After the DI we would carry out repairs and maintenance – allowing for the welcome visit of the NAAFI wagon. After dinner, if one was lucky enough to have his three aircraft serviceable by then, he would help a mate out, or do necessary tasks, such as servicing the starter-trolley. If ops were laid on, we would follow the armourers, checking the wiring on the bombs and plug them in. About an hour before take-off the Duty Electrician would be given the 'Mickey Mouse' – Bomb Selector and Distributor – settings and would have to rush round about fifteen planes to set and check the 'Mouse'.

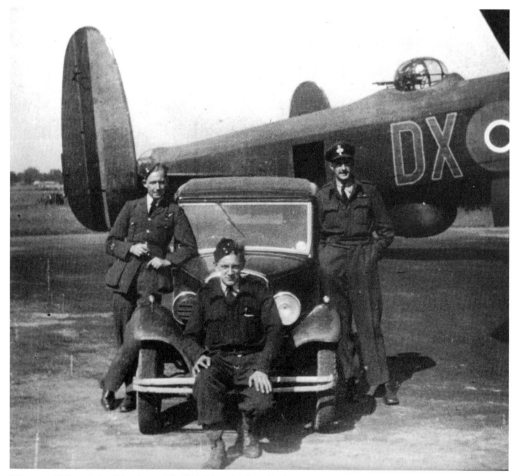

Warrant Officer John Woodrow CdeG(Bel.) and Flg Off Blank with Lancaster DX-S (J. Woodrow)

In support of the invading armies, raids against tactical targets were 'laid on' at short notice – and often changed or even 'scrubbed' just as suddenly. On one or two occasions the bombers were recalled while actually moving around the 'peri-track'. Often these sudden decisions were brought about by a change of circumstances in Normandy: smoke or cloud over the target area was quite intolerable when Allied troops were no more than 2,000 yards away.

Bomb loads were quite different for the varying objectives; after the hard graft of winching bombs up into the Lancaster's gaping bomb-bay, the armourers often had to unload and defuse them to be replaced by other weapons. Six tons of 'GP' 1,000-pounders would be rolled to the side of each dispersal and, perhaps, eighteen 500-pounders, more suitable 'treatment' for German armour, hoisted up in their stead.

Such was the load used on the night 7/8 June when Group was assigned to attack the 21st Panzer Division once more as their tanks lay concealed in the Forêt de Cerisy en route to the front. Each briefing brought variety, and an attack on the railway yards at Étampes followed.

A paper exercise during the summer seemed poor reward for loyalty when all the ground crews of the two squadrons were 'posted' to the nominal roll of Station Headquarters. The

LAC Silkstone and his Dodge oxygen truck (J.R. Bache)

purpose, no doubt, was to relieve squadron commanders and their office staff of considerable paperwork, for the Station personnel numbered around 3,000 by now. However, some – of both squadrons – had been with 57 since Methwold and the Wellington days and would not give in easily. They were, and remain, fiercely, 'Squadron Men': 'Once a Heinz Variety, always . . .'.

Though the scale was bigger, the tactical work was not dissimilar to that carried out by No. 57 Squadron in 1917/18. However, aerial warfare moved into a new dimension on 12 June when the enemy launched the first V1 'Flying Bomb' on London. Though Allied aircraft had made attacks on the storage and launching sites – usually referred to at Briefing as 'constructional works' – neither the crews nor the public at large knew of the existence of the crude but effective missiles until the first arrived.

A second, apparently more successful raid was carried out on the bridges over the Orne on 13/14 June. 'G-George', LM522, piloted by 57's 'A' Flt Cdr, Sqn Ldr D.I. Fairbairn, carried an extra 'bod' that night. Given the temporary identity of 'second engineer' for the occasion was Ronald Walker, *News Chronicle* air correspondent, and he provides an onlooker's view of the raid from the end of Briefing (which was attended by AOC, Group) to a safe return:

Over Caen Yesterday.

The AVM told them it had to be a good job; that the army was to be outside Caen watching the show. He asked them for accurate bombing of the Caen bridges, vital to the enemy for troop movement through the town.

It was still light when we gathered at the dispersal point for Lancaster G for George. The bomb doors yawned to reveal a maximum load of 1,000-pounders.

Engines were run up and equipment checked. With three-quarters of an hour to wait we stood around 'nattering'. The last cigarette smoked, a word from the pilot and we boarded the Lanc.

Gunners in a dog-fight among the Nissen huts of the very 'rural' 3 Site (Author)

[We taxied out, turned onto the runway, and soon], following the order to the flight engineer, 'Full power', came that always exciting moment. Almost 30 tons of aeroplane, carrying within its structure tons of petrol and many more tons of bombs, gathers itself and races past the runway lights at ever-increasing speed until the whole thing lifts away from the earth with an ease that can never cease to be rather surprising.

G for George ploughed smoothly through the night. Crossing the south coast our navigation lights went out, and we approached enemy France on a course which would avoid the assault area. After two or three changes of course we crossed the French coast. As we neared the target gun flashes and flak bursts in the surrounding sky increased. Except for one burst which came near but missed, the war avoided us.

Suddenly the glow of the coloured markers dropped by the Pathfinders became visible. Heavy flak was bursting far above us and lines of red balls came sailing up in a rather leisurely fashion to burst into stars. A bunch of searchlights illuminated the cloud base.

As G for George ran up to bomb cloud got in the way and we had to have another shot at it. 'Bomb doors open' came the call and we ran up to bomb with the markers clearly visible through drifting cloud. Quietly from the bomb-aimer, 'Steady, steady, steady. Hold it.' finally, 'Bombs gone'. The job was done.

To the north, slight hell was breaking loose, apparently Allied guns in the assault area. As we neared the French coast enemy fighters laid a trail of brilliant flares behind us on the cloud layer, beneath a half moon deeply tinged with red. Through and above cloud, G for George flew home to land in first light of a new day.

Fitters take time to pose atop a Packard Merlin – note 'paddle-blade' prop (Author)

The censor's pencil no doubt prevented the reporter from recording how, as they returned from this raid, the crews were obliged to cross the south coast at 10,000 feet, looking down at British light ack-ack firing at one of the flying bombs, easily visible by the flames from its tail-pipe.

On the night of the 14th No. 5 Group sent a force of 300 Lancasters to wipe out German transport and tanks alleged to be assembled in Aunay-sur-Odon. The end result, inevitably, was the total destruction of the little Norman town – some bombers were sent home with their bombs. It was established soon after that Aunay's destruction had been a tragic error, the result of a misinterpretation or other mix-up, for there was no military target there.

Despite resistance from HQ at High Wycombe, Bomber Command was tasked with the destruction of ten synthetic oil plants. On 21 June eighteen crews from 57 and nineteen from 630 were briefed to attack one such at Wesseling, some 20 miles south of Cologne. As was to be expected, the defences were at full strength and a heavy toll was imposed. In the moonlight of this, the shortest night, condensation trails showed where the bombers were to be found. Of the 120 Lancasters sent to this target, 36 were lost – just one fewer than East Kirkby's total effort. It is known that at least seven fell to the heavy barrage over the target; the remainder were victims of fighters; some of these were, in fact, FW190s armed with the 210-mm rockets they used with success against the USAAF by day.

Six of 57's aircraft failed to return. Flt Lt R.A.W. Beaumont DFC and Plt Offs Carr and Weightman were lost near the target, Flt Lt Bayley over Antwerp. Plt Off Guy died as his aircraft crashed near Hasselt. The bomb-aimer and engineer bailed out and were concealed by the Belgian Underground – the latter eventually married the daughter of the family that hid him!

Lancaster DX-A, ND471, arrived in January 1944, and was lost on 22 June, returning from her 41st operation (J. Lett)

Sgt Gren Hydes, wireless operator, was captured and put with an army POW work party. With them he was able to escape to the Russian lines and return home via the Middle East.

Luckiest of the crews reported 'Missing' was that aboard 'A-Able'. After at least three rockets had exploded underneath from successive attacks, three engines cut through fuel starvation. Five hundred gallons were jettisoned before Plt Off Nicklin brought off a successful ditching 70 miles off Great Yarmouth on the homeward leg, the whole crew being picked up by the Royal Navy.

No. 630 Squadron lost four Lancasters on the actual raid, the pilots concerned being Sqn Ldr A. Foster and Plt Offs T. Hart, R. Hooper and J. Smith. Additionally, 630's 'G-George' was again in trouble. The aircraft was attacked by a Ju88 and after a tremendous fusilade of cannon-shells from below, dropped 5,000 feet before the pilot, 'Blue' Rackley, and the engineer brought it under some semblance of control. The mid-upper gunner drove off the attacker but inspection revealed the havoc that had been wrought: a 6-feet hole in the front fuselage, rear turret smashed, H2S scanner and port elevator shot away. The tail unit controls were so damaged as to be almost ineffective. A rope was found from somewhere and the control column tied back.

After crossing the Suffolk coast, it was obvious to the captain that no landing was possible. Flying further inland, hopefully towards open country, he ordered the crew to bail out, and followed them. He was, himself, lucky, even though he was hit and injured by a train as he landed. He learned later that the rear gunner's parachute had been damaged beyond use and he had been 'doubled up' on the bomb-aimer's harness. But the gallant attempt was unsuccessful for the makeshift attachments failed and the gunner met the death he had so narrowly avoided when his original crew was lost in that fated first take-off in March.

Sgt 'Jock' Webster (back, right) with the armourers of 57's 'B' Flight. Roy 'Lofty' Jones is at the back, left (R.R. Jones)

It was East Kirkby's saddest night – and No. 5 Group's own 'Nuremburg'. Group and East Kirkby seemed to pause for breath. New aircraft arrived and new crews walked into the messes, feeling rather 'green' – they soon realized that many of those around them were little more experienced than they, despite having been 'blooded' by their first few ops.

It was a general rule that each new pilot should fly as 'second dickie' with an experienced crew for his first sortie. When a crew was first chosen to act as hosts in this way it was looked upon as a sort of 'coming-of-age', though the presence of the extra body in the cabin did not make things easier for the engineer, what spare space there was being used to stow two or three hundredweight of 'Window'.

During June, an aircraft of No. 630 Squadron returned to East Kirkby, though not having been 'missing' in the normal sense. Shortly after the infamous Nuremburg raid Plt Off Freddie Watts and his crew were posted to join No. 617 Squadron at Woodhall Spa. Left to make their own arrangements regarding transport, they promptly hijacked the aircraft they called their own, LE 'C-Charlie'. With her original nose-art, 'Conquering Cleo' flew as 'N-bar Nan' for months but was eventually missed and had to be returned!

There were no longer sergeant pilots on heavy bomber units, for the extended training at OTU, Heavy Conversion Unit and Lancaster Finishing School took more than a year and annual promotion would bring a Flt Sgt's crown and another shilling (5p) a day. A sudden decision in the summer of 1944 decreed that all captains of four-engined aircraft were to be of at least Flg Off rank, with an instant commission where necessary.

After Wesseling, the last two raids in June, on Ponnereval and Mimoyecques, were at somewhat reduced strength. Meanwhile, the ground crews worked hard to introduce 'Unit mods' to the new aircraft and the squadrons were soon back to full strength.

Crew of Lancaster DX-A on the afternoon before Wesseling (Author)

Lancaster DX-A, LM624, replaced the 'ditched' ND471 (Author)

The caves overlooking the River Oise at St Leu d'Esserant had been used by generations of mushroom-growers but had now become stores for V-weapons. Two attacks, on 4/5 and 7/8 July, were effective in the short term but cost Nos 57 and 630 Squadrons three and two aircraft respectively. The second of these raids was a disaster for No. 5 Group. Though there were nearly 600 bombers over France that night, their 228 Lancasters bore the brunt of the fighter defences and 31 were lost on the route to and from the target.

The one loss to No. 630 Squadron that night was a devastating blow, for the aircraft was flown by their CO, Wg Cdr 'Bill' Deas DFC, killed in action on his sixty-ninth operation. The first to fall on the attack was 57's 'G-George', the one that had taken the journalist to Caen. Now flown by Flg Off Stanley Findlay, she was shot down near Calais with the loss of all aboard. The Germans buried the remains of the crew by the spot where the aircraft had burnt out but the mayor of nearby Envermeu persuaded them to permit the pilot's body to be buried in the village churchyard. Only the local priest was allowed to attend along with the German burial party. A street nearby is now named 'Rue Findlay 8 Juillet 1944' and a memorial service is held at the crash site every November. Wg Cdr L.M. Blome-Jones DFC arrived shortly to assume command of No. 630 Squadron.

Calmont Chalindry was the next objective, followed by a raid on the railway yards at Nevers. On 18 July, thirty-five aircraft took off in daylight for yet another raid on the bridges at Caen and on strong-points established in the nearby steel works. It was teatime as the seventeen crews landed and some had to join others to make up the twenty crews to be briefed for another 'railway target', Revigny. This was a key junction of vital importance to the Germans and had been raided twice before. This time a direct route was taken but the raid was, apparently, anticipated. Casualties were high; of the 115 aircraft involved, 24 were lost, 4 from 630 and 1 from 57.

Flown by Flg Off John Bulcraig, only hours after returning from Caen, this 57 aircraft suffered a fighter attack.[2] As the port wing exploded and the fuselage burst into flames, only the navigator and the gunners managed to bail out. The rear gunner, Sgt Len Manning, was fortunate in escaping, jumping just in time with his parachute smouldering. He walked eight miles until picked up by the Resistance movement. After satisfying themselves that he was not a spy, they treated his burns and he was moved by various means to Paris, from where he was eventually liberated. His pilot and three comrades now lie in the cemetery at Basseville. Meanwhile, Sgt Albert de Bruin, a mid-upper gunner with 630 managed to bail out and escape captivity until he joined a Resistance group. They had, in fact, been to a rendezvous to meet an aircraft delivering weapons to a secret landing-ground. He stayed with the group for some months and, when the US Army arrived, wore GI combat kit for a couple of weeks.

A daylight raid on Thiverny followed,[3] then Courtrai and a gardening sortie off Kiel. But 'Bomber' Harris would not neglect what he saw as his prime objective, Germany, and a raid was mounted against Stuttgart on 24 July. 'J' Type incendiaries and blast bombs were used, creating fires visible for a hundred miles on the homeward journey. This cost 630 an aircraft, though another sortie, to St Nazaire, was carried out without loss – East Kirkby pitched thirty-one aircraft into battle that night.

Allied landings in the south of France were planned for August and the next raid was aimed at Givors, a vital railway junction in that area. As the force flew across France the weather deteriorated and they encountered severe storms. One of 57's planes was struck by lightning and made most of the journey on three engines. Enemy fighters found the bombers early on but the turbulence became so violent that they left them to it and the only defence met after that was a single light flak gun at Givors.

So intense did the storm become that marking was delayed and the constant flashes of

Wg Cdr W. Deas DFC with the crews of No. 630 Squadron, spring 1944 (Official, via J. Monk)

lightning revealed aircraft dangerously close and left the crews blinded. The Master Bomber's solution was simple: 'Switch your nav. lights on, chaps!' and so they circled the target for fifteen minutes with the lights providing safety from collision and a fine 'line to shoot' on their return: 'There we were . . .' The lonely flak gun banged away gamely but without effect and after the bombs had gone and the lights were switched off, the crews faced the elements to get home, static sparkling from guns, aerials and every projection on the plane.

With the onset of regular daylight raids the Group's aircraft were given a modified paint scheme. At East Kirkby, this took the form of various stripe patterns in red dope on fins and rudders, while squadron code letters were outlined in yellow. The purpose of the markings was to help in recognition as the Lancs climbed to assemble into a 'gaggle', as the rather loose formations were called.

The weather again took a hand when the bombers reached Cahagnes, close to the rubble of Aunay-sur-Odon, on 30 July. Early morning haze reaching 2,000 feet ruled out any chance of precision bombing just half a mile ahead of the British 2nd Army and the bombs were brought home. That afternoon No. 57 Squadron lost a brand-new aircraft with less than two hours flying

time logged when she failed to return from a test flight. It was believed that she came down in the Wash but no trace was ever found of her or her crew.

On the last day of July the squadrons joined a raid on the marshalling yard at Joigny La Roche, 75 miles south-east of Paris. It was a brilliant day and, with fighter escort now available from advance airstrips constructed in Normandy, might have been looked upon as 'a piece of cake'. Nevertheless, DX-Q, 'Fenland Queen', was lost with Flt Lt J.R.P. Spencer and four of her crew including 57's Engineer Leader, Flt Lt R.T. Clarke DFM, on his fiftieth operation. Only Sgt J. Grice, wireless operator, and the navigator, Plt Off N. Hughes-Games, RCAF, escaped, though the latter died in captivity.

July had been even busier than June and No. 57 Squadron's ORB sums up the month's work well:

During the month the Squadron operated on 20 occasions; 17 night and 3 daylight raids were made, in which 200 sorties were flown. Ten (*sic* – seven) aircraft failed to return.

The flying times for these operations amounted to Lancaster Mk I, 457.4 hours and Lancaster Mk III, 668.15 hours, a total of 1,125.55 operational flying hours for the month.

Steve Nunns' 'extended' crew with 'D-Dog' (J. Elliott)

An anonymous No. 57 Squadron Lancaster but a veteran, as is revealed by the heavy lead deposits on the upper wing surfaces (IWM CH12971)

The author, seated outside Hut 13, 3 Site, 1944
(Author)

Small tactical targets in support of our advancing armies and others against V1 sites and dumps were chosen for the attention of No. 57 Squadron with others from No. 5 Group. Possibly the most interesting was the now-famous attack on the Monteville Steel Works at CAEN, 2,000 yards in advance of British troops and the attacks on the V1 storage sites in the caves at St Leu d'Esserant. Three runs were made to STUTTGART and one to KIEL, just to keep the 'home fires burning'. Six railway junctions received our attention and helped to add to the already mounting chaos on the railway communications in western Europe. . . .

Although ten crews were lost during the month, the Squadron lived up to its motto 'Corpus Non Animum Muto' by successfully completing more operations in one month than has ever been attempted before. For their invaluable work in this achievement the ground staff are to be highly commended.

Non-operational flying for the month amounted to 268.35 hours day and 60.15 hours night, bringing the total for all flying up to 1,454.45 hours, an average of 81 hours per aircraft.

No. 630 Squadron took part in all of these operations, but lost nine aircraft.

With operations still being 'laid on' at short notice, night or day, the work of the ground crew was certainly worthy of commendation. Sweating on the wings or roasting in the heat of the fuselage that had stood in the sun all day, the metal skin too hot to touch, they did their maintenance tasks, then bombed-up and refuelled for a night raid. Next morning they began again, often in a hurry. The changing of ammunition belts from day to night tracer, or vice versa, was just another of the time-consuming chores involved.

Lancaster LE-F, Spirit of Canada *(R.D. Gale)*

Hazen Long, RCAF, flew the last nineteen ops of his tour in 'Fox' (R.D. Gale)

Operations continued to be planned, changed, cancelled or reinstated. The most notable of the 'scrubbed' ops was Operation Thunderclap. The crews were called to a 'pre-briefing' one afternoon. The Base Commander told of the projected mass attack to be made next morning. No. 55 Base, East Kirkby, was to lead No. 5 Group, which, in turn, was to head a massive turnout of the whole of Bomber Command, accompanied by all the 'heavies' the USAAF could muster. The Station Commander proudly announced that the senior squadron, No. 57, followed by 207 (Spilsby) and 630 were to be in the van. Reveille would be at 01.00 hours. Target, route, timing, etc., would be detailed at Briefing, 02.00 hours.

In the event, reveille was forgotten, and so was Thunderclap; second thoughts prevailed and the plans came to nought, as ACM Harris explains in his book *Bomber Offensive*:

. . . in the late summer of 1944, when the German army was in headlong retreat from France and it seemed conceivable that the war might end at any moment, there was a plan to carry out a vast Anglo-American air attack on Berlin in daylight; the idea was that this might cause the German Government to panic at a critical moment. General Doolittle* and I and our staffs examined the final plan together in the Operations Room. The routes were decided and the whole operation pretty well cut and dried when I discovered that the Americans, whose long-range fighters were required to protect Bomber Command's striking force as well as their Fortresses, were unable to raise enough fighters to give what I considered adequate cover for our aircraft during such a deep penetration of Germany. The greater part of our striking force was unable to fly in formation and in an operation involving the whole or most of the force the bomber stream was inevitably very long, stretching to sixty miles or more, so that a large fighter force had always to be assembled when we attacked a German target in daylight. There had been some misunderstanding about this. . . .

Although Jimmy Doolittle did his utmost, as always, to meet our requirements I had to refuse to subject my force to a risk far greater than usual – I had in mind our obsolete .303 calibre defensive armament – the whole operation was therefore cancelled.

Bomber Command was being called upon almost daily to carry out attacks upon the various sites used, or intended, for the storage and launching of V-weapons. The principal enemy defence encountered on these occasions was flak with extremely efficient ranging equipment. The 'Daylight Window' dropped to counter enemy radar took the form of 5-feet long strips which looked very spectacular in the sunlight but seemed to be no great deterrent.

On 1 August, an afternoon sortie was mounted on such a site at Siracourt but the raid was a failure owing to cloud over the target. Another, to a flying-bomb site at Trossey St Maximin a couple of days later was met with an extremely accurate flak barrage. Several planes were damaged but all got home, as was the case when the raid was repeated next day. Two more V-weapon sites, St Leu d'Esserant and l'Ile Adam were fitted in between other French targets: heavy raids on Sequeville and Châtellerault and a lighter one on the port of Bordeaux.

On a daylight raid on the V1 store at l'Ile Adam, north of Paris, it was noted that the flak was lighter. For the first time since D-Day, German fighters were out in some strength – estimated at up to thirty Me109s. No. 630 Squadron lost an aircraft, while 57's 'V-Victor' was in a long running battle with one of the Messerschmitts. Despite two gun-turrets being put out of action, Wg Cdr Humphreys evaded attack after attack until the enemy was almost out of fuel and had to retire.

---

*   Commanding US Army Air Force bomber force.

Another view of 'Fox' with half a Lancaster in the background. LE-F was destined to be lost in December 1944 (R.D. Gale)

Flt Lt Nick Nicklin DFC, RNZAF, and crew pose for an 'end of tour' photo (Author)

Eighteen of East Kirkby's Lancs took part in another raid on Givors on 11/12 August and next night, seventeen took off for a further sortie against Brunswick. Just after they left, seven more crews were briefed for a hastily mounted raid on a crossroads where German troops were frantically attempting to escape from the Falaise pocket as two US armies swooped in for the kill. Attacks on Brest and Deelen followed on successive nights.

Flt Lt Eric Blanchard DFC was no stranger to No. 57 Squadron, having completed his first tour with them. Now, posted in to fill the vacant Engineer Leader's post, he was eager to find out what these daylight operations were about. Opportunity seemed to arise straight away; on 16 August a crew was short of an engineer so he 'put himself on the list' and joined them.

It was a night raid and Stettin was attacked in a complex operation. Sixteen East Kirkby aircraft joined in a Group Main Force raid on the city from 17,200–20,000 feet without loss. Six other crews were among those briefed to lay mines from 250–300 feet along a path of flame floats laid in the harbour. They met withering light flak head on and two were obliged to abandon their mission through damage; another, flown by 57's Flt Lt Scutt failed to return. The flight engineer, Malcolm Crapper, recalls that his pilot attempted to climb from their operating height as the plane burst into flames. The engineer, bomb-aimer and mid-upper gunner managed to bail out, but the rest perished. Crapper came down in the sea and swam ashore to safety – and captivity.

Meanwhile, flying immediately behind, a witness. Eric Blanchard takes up the story:

We are to orbit at about 500 feet to await our PFF. Away to the south are searchlight cones above Stettin; Main Force have started their bombing, a sight we have never seen before from this height.

Parachute flares light our target, the partially enclosed waters, and we see light flak firing at someone at almost sea level. The voice of the Controller comes over the RT: 'I'm going in, chaps. Sorry; take over, best of luck.' There he is, in flames. We fly in, heading for the channel. Thirty degree flap (to decrease speed), bomb doors open . . . committed to straight and level . . . flak seems to be coming from all over the place – it looks parallel to the sea and appears to be concentrating on a Lanc in front. Mines gone . . . doors closed and we put the throttles right through the gate and go like hell, firstly to clear the land ahead, then to reach 20,000 feet. It was slow, until we remembered to raise the flaps!

The Germans were still hanging on to French Atlantic ports. Cut off, the troops there were being ignored, but the value to German naval forces was another thing. Oil storage tanks at Bordeaux were the target when five aircraft from each unit joined in a daylight attack on 11 August. No. 630's ORB recorded that the loads carried comprised six 1,900 lb Special Armour Piercing, fused .025 seconds: 'these had not been used for some considerable time and caused some surprise when brought into the daylight'. It was also recorded that 630's 'I-Item', piloted by Flg Off J. Bolton, was seen heading north-east after the attack, losing height from the formation.

No. 57 Squadron joined the No. 5 Group attack on enemy warships in Brest harbour on 20/21 August. They suffered no loss but as the weather 'clamped down' across Britain there was a rush to get back safely. Some managed to get into England's most southerly airfield, Predannack, atop the cliffs on the Lizard, while others made a dash for Woodvale, near Southport.

Quite unexpectedly, good news. For the ground crews, restoration of their leave entitlement. For the aircrews, tour duration was cut back to thirty operations. Subsequently, a number of crews found themselves 'Tour Expired'.

The mining/bombing raid on Stettin was copied twice towards the end of the month, the target Königsberg, vital to the Germans as the Russians drew closer, now only 100 miles away. Enormous damage was done to the harbour area, though the second raid took place in severe thunderstorms. However, these 2,000 mile round trips were not without cost, for 57 lost two crews.

After three months, Operation Chastise, the attacks on the flying-bomb sites, came to a close,

Ground crew on 'the flights' (F. Beasley)

the last V-1 from France landing on Britain on 2 September. By now the permanent sites had been overrun by Allied forces. Bomber Command had carried out 12,000 sorties on these installations.[5]

Despite the distances, the raids in support of the Red Army could be considered tactical rather than strategic attacks. Bomber Command's contribution to the assault on Fortress Europe and the battles that followed would not be forgotten. Again and again they were called upon in their powerful supporting role. Nevertheless, as autumn and the long nights approached, Harris was looking once more towards what he always considered his prime target, the Reich.

Wg Cdr J.E. Grindon DFC assumed command of No. 630 Squadron in September. Two other new arrivals to the squadron presented themselves before 'A' Flt Cdr, Sqn Ldr Millichap.[5] 'What are your names?' he asked. 'Monk and Nunns? That's all we need – a Holy War!'

The squadrons were steadily gaining in strength as a result of the welcome cut in the losses. This did, however, mean that each crew would operate less often and tours would take much longer. Just as squadron strength grew, so did No. 5 Group. Its bomb-carrying capacity was now such that they usually operated independently. It had its own Pathfinder squadrons, though any No. 5 Group squadron might find itself called upon to take part in this work and their commanders were called upon in turn to fly as Master Bomber.

Like all new pilots, Flg Off Jerry Monk was eager to have an aircraft he could call his own. A new 'G-George' arrived and no one seemed to be interested, so he laid claim to her. The reluctance was soon explained – 'Georges' never seemed to last long. However, he took her over and, apart from radar failure on the first trip, found her to be first-class.

When an attack on Darmstadt was planned, sections of the Group were allotted aiming points

No. 57's 'A' Flight ground crew 'at home' (F. Beasley)

in the industrial area, each to be bombed from a different direction and each aircraft to 'overshoot' the markers by a given number of seconds. The target was devastated, though 630's ORB recorded that the squadron was in the third wave and 'orbitted for twenty minutes trying to run over the target on H2S. The Controller was not heard at all, so they bombed on the fires below.'

Bremerhaven was next to suffer in this way and heavy raids against a number of German cities followed: Stuttgart, Mönchengladbach and Karlsruhe among them.

Soon in action, the other of 630's 'Holy Pair', Flg Off Steve Nunns found trouble en route for Kaiserslautern. The port inner engine caught fire suddenly and the flames began to spread. He ordered the crew to abandon. Sgt Jim Elliott could not escape from his rear turret until released by his colleague. He was last to leave, urged on by the skipper, who engaged the auto-pilot and prepared to follow. The flames seemed to abate; he got back into his seat but the fire, just feet away seemed to worsen and again he prepared to leave. Still undecided, he looked at the charts and worked out a direct course for base. By now, the flames were much less and he made his mind up and took over from 'George'.

He made his lonely journey home and called 'Silksheen', the East Kirkby call-sign. They learned of his full bomb load and told him to get rid of it, so he headed for the jettison area in the North Sea. Over base once more, he was given permission to land and accomplished the by no means inconsiderable task of putting 'D-Dog' back on the ground in one piece single-handed.

He ate a lonely breakfast, full of concern for his crew. The bomb-aimer and Jim Elliott had

weddings planned for the next month. He had no need to worry. Jim Elliott dodged Germans –
and suspicious French farmers – swam a canal and made contact with the Maquis who passed
him on to the US troops. Two days later he was back in England, ready to claim a record for a
speedy return. The first person he saw as he dropped off the Dakota was his fellow gunner!
Within a week the crew were reunited. No. 630's ORB note was short, both in words and fact:
'The pilot returned alone. The remainder of the crew returned the same day'!

On 14/15 October Group turned its attention on Brunswick. Using the, by now, well-proven
'sector' method, the city received 847 tons in a highly concentrated raid – a bonus, for such a
speedy attack gave the roaming fighters less time to seek out a target.

Twice in October the bombers were called on to breach the sea wall at Westkappelle so as to
flood the Dutch island of Walcheren where enemy troops were putting up a stiff resistance
against the Canadian Army. East Kirkby was out in force on 19/20 October, when a total of
forty-one bombers were sent to Nuremburg. Another sortie against Walcheren followed a
'maximum effort' against the Norwegian port of Bergen. November began with two heavy
raids, against Homberg and Düsseldorf. Next an attack on Ladbergen, actually a village by a
strategic point on the Dortmund–Ems canal, a prime route for the transport of armaments.

Throughout October, mining and raids on canals were priorities, and when the Mittelland
Canal was hit it was drained for a mile, stranding all the barges along its length. At the end of
the month the ribbons across the map in the Briefing Rooms were again pinned towards its
north-east corner, the target being the U-boat pens in the Norwegian port of Trondheim.
However, the raid was no great success, for visibility was very poor and on return the aircraft
had to be diverted to Carnaby, Yorkshire, the nearest airfield with the fog-dispersing FIDO
equipment. (To land amidst its flames was a new experience for most.)

No. 630's 'E-Easy' was unable to take off on schedule and, as a result of trying to make up
time, used excessive fuel and ran out just short of the coast by the Humber estuary. The pilot,
Flg Off Ross Flood, RNZAF, attempted a ditching but the aircraft hit a sandbank and was lost
with all on board.

The raids against Gravenhorst and Harburg had also cost a plane each but the work during
October and November had been carried out with much lower losses than before. Nevertheless,
though only five aircraft had been lost in three months, every loss was a loss too many, bringing
tragedy and worry to many families.

NOTES TO CHAPTER 8

1   The defensive 'corkscrew' used by the bomber crews was not, of course, a corkscrew or barrel-roll as performed
by fighter or aerobatic aircraft. The manoeuvre consisted of alternate dives and climbs to port and starboard, so
presenting an ever-changing target to a pursuing fighter, but continuing along the same course.

2   This Lancaster was one of five shot down by Luftwaffe pilot Herbert Altner in the space of just half an hour.

3   Early in July, 57's 'B' Flt Cdr 'Drew' Wyness took on an old chum, Wg Cdr Guy Gibson VC DSO DFC, on an
NFT with him. Despite being 'grounded' from operations by Harris himself, 'Gibbo' returned later and went on 'just
one more', the Thiverny raid, as second pilot in 630's 'N-Nan' flown by Sqn Ldr Miller. This was the last operation to
be entered into his remarkable logbook: 'Daylight operations, Thiverny, nr Creil, 25 m NW Paris. Successful aiming
point, Mod Flak.'

4   From the Air Ministry came a signal to all squadrons involved: 'The continuous and heavy bombing of the sites
imposed on the enemy a prolonged and unwelcome delay in the launching of his campaign [and] effectively limited the
scale of effort which he was able to make.'

5   Capt Millichap of BOAC made a noteworthy flight in October 1958, when he flew the world's first ever jet
airliner, the DH Comet 4, on her maiden transatlantic service flight.

CHAPTER 9

The Last Year of War

Despite the undoubted advantages enjoyed by the German fighter pilots with their highly organized 'boxes', airborne radar and the *Schrägemusik* cannon, the East Kirkby crews had had a little respite. It did not last. With the approach of winter, crews began to face their other hazard, the weather.

The squadrons' first raid in December 1944, on the 4th/5th, was aimed at Heilbron. No. 57's 'J-Jig', flown by Lt P. Becker, SAAF, was lost that night, Vic Tomei, the bomb-aimer, being the sole survivor:

> Turning for home, we were attacked. Our port wing and engines caught fire, the flames could not be extinguished and orders were given to bail out. I jettisoned the hatch but the aircraft started to spin. We straightened out and I was thrown out feet first, catching the back edge of the hatch before I fell. My parachute opened but I began to spin, being held by one clip only. I corrected this and landed in a farmyard where I was captured by a group of armed villagers.

From East Kirkby forty aircraft were involved that night and it was only through good fortune that losses were not greater. Two of 630's, flown by Flt Lts Frank Jones and Jock Baugh, RAAF, were struck by incendiary bombs dropped from above. Some were found embedded in the wing of one, while the latter pilot was injured when a 4-pounder came through the cabin canopy and struck his arm.

Two nights later two of 57's aircraft were lost attacking Giessen. Flg Off W. Riddell and four of his crew were killed. Sgt J. Turner became a prisoner of war, unaware of the fate of his colleague, the bomb-aimer, Flt Sgt Neil McGladrigan, RAAF, who was soon captured and handed over to the German police. He was kept in their custody until 10 December when he was taken into a forest, shot in the temple and buried in a shallow grave.

Among other operations early in the month were three 'dam-busting' raids on Urftdam. The purpose of the raids was to release the waters of the River Urft early so that they could not be loosed upon approaching US troops, but, as was found on the original, more famous exploits, dams do not give way easily. No. 57 lost a crew in a tragic collision over the target on the third, still unsuccessful, attempt.

Two more aircraft out of eighteen were lost to 57 on a raid on Munich. Among the pilots that night was Flg Off Les Barnes, 'home' from Stuttgart at last after a ten-month journey that had taken him through France and over the Pyrenees via the famous 'Comet' escape route. It had not been forgotten that he 'owed' a further twenty-six ops – he fulfilled his 'contract'.

For the rest of the month, some of the targets allotted, mainly mining, were a bit nearer home, with the exception of Gdynia and Politz. On return from each of these in fog and frost, many aircraft were diverted to the giant emergency runway at Woodbridge in Suffolk and it was over a week before all got back to base.

Snow abounded; it was a white and bitterly cold Christmas in the poorly heated Nissen huts but it was celebrated as near to the traditions as circumstances allowed. For the aircrews who had missed out on the operations or had managed to get 'home', it was a better Christmas than for those who had been diverted elsewhere without 'small kit' for a shave (or even without money, if orders had been strictly followed).

Jerry Monk and some of his crew with 'G-George', Christmas 1944 (J. Monk)

'Holiday' or not, it was soon over and two crews from each squadron were ordered off on Boxing Day to bomb the German ground forces who were mounting an assault at St Vith. This, in fact, was the opening phase of the Nazis' last ditch Battle of the Bulge.

One of 630's crews, captained by Jerry Monk, was newly back from Woodbridge. Their enforced abstinence made them favourites and he set the crew to de-icing a prepared aircraft. Just before take-off the wireless operator heard that his parents had been bombed out by a flying-bomb – still being launched from the air. Reg Fletcher, W/Op with Steve Nunns' crew, took his place.

Monk continues:

The Intelligence Officer told us that the target was St Vith and we could make our own arrangements. I picked a bombing height of 14,000 feet and flew straight to the target – tank concentrations in the Ardennes battle. We made our run over the battlefield in brilliant sunshine to find all the Halifaxes that Bomber Command possessed crossing at a tangent, about 6,000 feet above. Thousand pounders and Window fell around us like tinsel but all the bombs missed us. This time we were diverted to St Eval in Cornwall.

Reg Fletcher has his own memories of the trip. He too had been stuck at Woodbridge. Though there was a wonderful runway, long and wide, facilities were poor. St Eval was even less comfortable and the intrusive 'glamour boys' of Bomber Command were offered nothing. Two days later the weather cleared and they were able to escape. Like Predannack, the runway was atop the cliffs and a Lancaster take-off was rather like leaving an aircraft carrier, for it

Sergeants' Mess, well decorated for Christmas – have all the crews been diverted? (L. Wakerell)

simply fell over the end and down towards the sea. Monk climbed a little then circled and made a low run over the field, giving the crew opportunity to give Flying Control their opinion of 'St Evil' with the two-fingered 'Agincourt salute'. However, the telephone is quicker than a Lanc and Monk had an uncomfortable interview with the CO on return.

Bad visibility returned by 30 December and despite all airfield lighting being turned on, a B-17 of the USAAF, which had struggled to cross the North Sea, failed to reach the runway and crashed on the hill. All aboard were killed. Despite the fog, operations continued to the New Year, with further attacks on German troops in the Ardennes and more mine-laying. It began to clear on 1 January, in time to begin day and night raids on the canals, and a busy week followed as a variety of targets were attacked.

On 8 January, a heavy raid was mounted against Munich – twenty-nine crews were briefed. Jerry Monk flew 'G-George' back from yet another diversion in time for her to be serviced and bombed up, but the CO decided that his place should be taken by George 'Billy' Billings. A engine cut out straight after take-off and the bombs were jettisoned. On return, the Lanc bounced as it touched down, the other engine on the same side cut and the plane cartwheeled on to the runway. Several of the crew were killed but Billings was thrown clear, still in his seat but severely injured – he lost an arm. It would have been LE-G's seventeenth operation; she had had a longer run than all the other 'Georges' but 630 never had another.

Politz, Merseburg and an oil plant at Brux followed. On the latter raid, a pilot of 57, Flg Off Jerrold Jackson, RAAF, lost an engine on the outward leg, but, as his citation for an 'immediate' DFC records: 'this officer did not hesitate to continue his mission. Some height

'Jock' Hoare DFC, RAAF, with Lancaster 'L-Love', NN774 (D. Brown)

Flt Lt Hoare (left, holding a practice bomb), and crew (D. Brown)

had been lost as the target was reached but he made an accurate attack in the face of considerable enemy fire. He afterwards flew his aircraft safely back to base.'

From 17 January Lincolnshire lay all but buried in snow. All hands to the shovels – the airfield must be kept serviceable. At this time, a number of aircrew cadets had been posted in to do a variety of 'odd jobs' about the station while awaiting their chance of training at the Central Navigation School in Canada.

One, Alan Turner, describes how small groups of these cadets were allocated to different sections. His memories provide an insight into some of the tasks that went on quite unnoticed, essential though they were. His first few weeks were under the direction of Flying Control.

As winter set in with a vengeance this was primarily a matter of keeping the operational runway visible: well before ETA of the returning aircraft we went out with a lorry load of 'goosenecks' – paraffin flares like long watering cans. As the lorry drove slowly down the centre of the runway we had to dash out to the edge to place a flaming gooseneck beside each of the lights whose faint glow could just be seen beneath the snow. I do not remember snow clearance; my memory is of a runway that looked like a busy main road. Every available vehicle, from petrol bowsers to the CO's car had been pressed into service to drive up and down to compact the snow sufficiently for the aircraft to land.

I next had a spell in the bomb dump, mainly screwing pistols into the noses of the bombs as required and fitting the little red propellers that would arm them as they fell away. Other colours were sometimes used, indicating that some type of trick fuse had been installed to make things interesting for the Jerry bomb disposal people. There were left-hand threads and some that were sensitive to the heat of the hand. I was none too happy when handling these, not that there was much heat in our hands, working in the open in mid-winter.

It was disconcerting to see how the bomb dump crews treated their job. 1,000-pounders

Snowballs were something new to the 'Aussies' (Mrs K. Rowland)

were lifted by mobile crane, three or four at a time, supported on an 'L'-shaped hook rather than a 'J'. Inevitably, I saw one coming adrift one day, and ducked behind the nearest solid object. There was a dull thump and I got to my feet to discover that my 'solid object' was the end one of a stack of 4,000-pounders!

The weather improved with February's arrival and for most of the month the targets continued to be those so often on the 'menu' that winter, the canals, lifelines to the German forces in the east. Between came Karlsruhe, Politz – from which raid a plane was lost – Rositz, Bohlen and, on 13/14 February, one other, Dresden.

Dresden. What can be said that has not already been said – not always truthfully. The undoubtedly beautiful city was bombed three times in all, including an attack on the following day – 14 February – by the USAAF. For those who took part in these raids Dresden was just another target. This huge city was plainly a major rail junction serving the eastern front and a vast manufacturing centre, surely turning out more than china shepherdesses.

Tragic? Murderous? Of course. There can be no other kind of air raid. Some, with all the advantages of hindsight, claim that the war was nearly over. Those Londoners who suffered the onslaught of seventy carelessly directed V2 rockets that very week might question such a statement. There are others who seem to take the view that the raid should have been carried out with a little restraint. However, the bomber forces surely cannot be blamed for doing their job too well. Over Guernica, Warsaw, Rotterdam, then London, Coventry, Norwich, they had been shown how to wage total war; nothing was said about restraint. Their supporters, at least 95 per

Plt Off Harris, RNZAF, and crew (T. Lockett)

cent of the British public, needed some way of fighting back and from the days of Dunkirk until June 1944; there had been no other way.

With so much activity in the skies above Lincolnshire, accidents were inevitable, though thankfully quite rare. In the early hours of 2 March, 57's ND572 collided with ME473 of No. 207 Squadron from nearby Spilsby. Fourteen men died as the planes crashed together into Ruskington Fen, near Sleaford.[1] Among the seven aboard ND572 was Hunter Aitken, one of the aircrew cadets. His friend, Alan Turner, recalls 'Jimmy' Aitken's delight at being invited to join the training flight and the shock at seeing his empty bed next morning.

March continued as February had ended, with a raid on the Dortmund–Ems canal but, as the station's twenty-eight aircraft returned, a Bandit found his way onto the circuit – which was less than 20 miles from the coast. 'Scram' action was taken immediately; all airfield lights were switched off and approaching aircraft were warned to divert, which they did effectively. However, the enemy was not to be denied a target and the MT Section and 57's Briefing Room were raked with cannon shells. The team awaiting the return of the crews for their debrief were caught in the fire. Five were severely wounded, including the WAAF CO, and the Signals Analysis Officer who subsequently died of his wounds.

Two nights later, East Kirkby hit back by sending their heaviest force for some months,

Flt Lt Neil Roberts, RAAF, and crew (Mrs K. Rowland)

thirty-eight aircraft, to Bohlen. They returned safely, but 630 lost a plane over Würzburg. No. 57 lost two more planes in the month, one on Harburg, and one on a further raid on Bohlen (the squadron's last operational loss). This was a tragic night from the start, for DX-Y was seen to veer away from its take-off path, losing height. She crashed on the end of a bungalow in the village of Stickney, close by.

Armament Officer Flt Lt John MacBean had a motorbike and was among the first on the scene: 'There was fire all around. A number of bombs had exploded (breaking windows as far away as Skegness) and ammunition was "crackling off" in the flames.' He helped to rescue two badly injured crew members from the rear fuselage as the fire rapidly took over, but could not locate the 'Cookie'. After removing the detonators from some of the bombs – one had split open and its contents were adding to the inferno – he advised the Station Commander that evacuation was essential.

I returned at first light and found the pilot's body some way away from the still-smouldering wreckage with its well-cooked Cookie below. It would have been capable of flattening the entire village.

A later memory was of the brood of day-old chicks that were running around amid the flames. Also, two days later he discovered that the heat-sensitive detonators were still in his trouser pocket!

Flg Off Les Jacobs, and crew (Mrs K. Rowland)

No. 630 Squadron was honoured during the month when the king approved the award of a Squadron Badge. It took as its emblem the Lancaster rose for the only aircraft type the squadron ever flew. The motto 'Nocturna Mors' translates as 'Death by Night'.

Other quite heavy attacks were mounted against Essen, Dortmund, Lutzkendorf, Würzburg and Hamburg but the last raid of the month was very different. By 23 March the British Army had reached the banks of the Rhine and was preparing to cross. Operation Varsity, Bomber Command's mass attack on Wesel, just 700 yards away, made their crossing into something of a formality. General Montgomery's message to ACM Harris next day read:

> My grateful appreciation for the quite magnificent co-operation you have given us in the Battle of the Rhine. The bombing of Wesel last night was a masterpiece and was the decisive factor, making possible our entry into the town before midnight.

A daylight raid on Noordhausen, followed by night raids on Lutzkendorf and Leipzig, started April off in much the same manner, but it was a bad start for No. 630 Squadron. One aircraft crashed and two failed to return from Leipzig, their last losses to enemy action.

East Kirkby suffered a severe blow on the evening of 17 April as preparations were in hand for a raid on a target near the Czech border. At 17.45 hours bombing-up was nearly finished. From, perhaps, a petrol spillage, fire broke out on the dispersal used by 57's 'U-Uncle'. The fire-tender arrived promptly but unfortunately, just as two 1,000 lb bombs exploded. A fireman and a private of the Pioneer Corps[2] were killed instantly. Although injured, another fireman, LAC William Thaxton, managed to get his wounded corporal to a place of comparative safety; others, too, risked life and limb in rescue work.

Flg Off Jimmy Wallace, RNZAF (centre), and crew (Mrs K. Rowland)

Lancaster 'Q-Queen', about to be bombed up for the attack on Leipzig, 10 April 1945. A. Ricketts, F/E and R. Haslam, Navigator (A.H. Ricketts)

Capt Desmond Reynolds, SAAF, and crew (Mrs K. Rowland)

In a short time the flames had spread to two more aircraft and soon the bombs on these began to explode. Despite falling from his motorbike as he rushed through the gate by the guardroom, John MacBean arrived. A hangar nearby was being used as a store for some 300 tons of incendiary bombs and he could see, through the shattered panels, that one or two 4-pounders were alight. He ran to them with a drum filled with sand. Yet another explosion blew him along the hangar but, by chance, extinguished the flames as well.

Explosions continued as Flg Off Grebby, the Station Fire Officer, arrived at the scene which, fortunately, was on the far side of the airfield, away from the village. By the time he arrived an ambulance attendant and another airman had been killed and more had been injured. Tremendous bravery was displayed by many that evening as Grebby joined in the rescue work. Among these were Flg Off Gott GM, Cpls Raymond Forster and Leslie Friswell and LAC Frederick Brown, who worked on despite their injuries. Meanwhile, Courtney Grebby approached a body to recover it, ignoring warnings that a 4,000 lb 'Cookie' lay nearby. A further explosion hurled him away, severely injured – his life was saved by application of a tourniquet made from the Station Commander's braces.

A fourth Lancaster was alight as fire crews and ambulances began to arrive from the nearby stations of Coningsby and Spilsby, but little could be done other than wait until after the casualties had been taken away.[3]

Electrician Denis Howell was setting the 'Mickey Mouse' again that evening:

Electrical and instrument stores (Author)

Suddenly the whole Squadron seemed to blow up. I helped tow some planes away before we were told that the aerodrome was to be evacuated.

The bombs loaded for the operation, all HE, had been fused with half and one hour delay pistols, all liable to join in a chain reaction. Eventually the thunderous explosions seemed to come to an end but .303 ammunition continued to crackle as the fires burned themselves out.

By now 630's aircraft had been left where they stood, all flying operations having been abandoned, and it was a long, anxious night for all at East Kirkby, service people and villagers alike.

The dispersal where the original outbreak had occurred was close by the farmhouse and other buildings of Hagnaby Grange (unoccupied since the airfield was built). At first light it could be seen that they were half demolished, tiles from the roofs lying scattered among the torn aluminium, vast boulders of concrete and, worst of all, many live bombs that had been thrown around at random. The first thing to be done in the cold light of day was for the armourers to inspect each of these, looking for the staining in the fuse that would indicate that it had been activated by the disturbance. All were found to be in order with the exception of two or three that lay in the bottom of a deep crater. A crane was sent for but before it arrived the crater was enlarged by the rogue 1,000-pounders, fortunately without causing injury.

In all, besides the five fatalities, fourteen, including some civilians, had been hurt in the explosions; the injuries of several were described as severe. Four aircraft had been totally destroyed and ten others suffered heavy damage, many being written off. The damage to the

Ruins of Hagnaby Grange farm (Official, via J. MacBean)

airfield was mainly confined to the hardstandings and perimeter track on 57 Squadron's (eastern) side and it took eight days for 'Works and Bricks' to get that part of the airfield back into some sort of usable condition.

A raid planned against Flensberg on 23 April was abandoned, but on 25 April five crews from each squadron joined in a bombing raid that must have caught everyone's fancy – target, Berchtesgaden. They were to bomb the SS barracks and, close by, the luxury homes of Herman Goering and Martin Bormann. However, Hitler had chosen well when seeking a site for his 'Eagle's Nest'. All aircraft returned safely but damage to the objectives was limited by the difficulties presented by the surrounding mountains. (With immaculate timing, Eric Blanchard completed his fiftieth 'op' and second tour as he touched down.)

This turned out to be East Kirkby's last bombing raid. That evening eight planes took off to lay mines in Oslo Fjord – the 'Onions' area. When Flg Off 'Jake' Jacobs of 630, followed by Flg Off Meeks of 57, landed at 03.00 hours on the morning of 26 April they brought East Kirkby's offensive part in the Second World War to a close.

The fighting in Europe continued for nearly a fortnight as the squadrons joined in Operation Exodus, the repatriation of the thousands of Allied prisoners of war. The satisfying work was not even interrupted on 8 May, VE Day, and half a dozen crews carried on as the rest of the Station paraded to hear Winston Churchill's speech over the tannoy system. Fifty years on, the celebrations held that evening were still remembered locally as 'quite a party'.

'Exodus' continued until the end of May, with Nos 57 and 630 Squadrons transporting over 1,800 'ex-kriegies' to the reception centres in the south. One of these, an air gunner with 57, related the story of his interrogation at Dulagluft: the Luftwaffe officer looked at the report that told him the identity of the aircraft wreckage with its 'DX' code. He smiled disarmingly and offered a cigarette: 'How's Taafe?' Grp Capt Taafe, East Kirkby's much respected Station

Chaos remained (Official, via J. MacBean)

DX-P was scrapped where she stood (Official, via J. MacBean)

A new 'Q-Queen', replacing LM653, lost over Halle (A.H. Ricketts)

Commander was undoubtedly known as 'Groupie' but never by his surname. The only person the gunner could remember of that name was the Welsh rigger on his Lancaster! There was not much to be said after that.

Further trips over the continent were known as 'Cook's Tours' when a few lucky ground crew members, men and women, were given a low-level look at the destruction their efforts had brought about on the Ruhr factories.[4]

Many bomb disposal flights were carried out to get rid of unstable or out-dated bombs in the North Sea. It was on one such errand that 630's 'R-Robert' was lost. Following radio confirmation that her bombs had been dropped, no more was heard, though crews from both squadrons made a widespread search. Soon after this the squadron suffered another inexplicable loss when LE-S, a brand-new aircraft engaged on an exercise, was seen to emerge from low cloud and plunge to the ground near Wednesford, Staffordshire, with the loss of all on board.

There were rumours that 630 was to be moved to Skellingthorpe, but as the Canadian and Australian members began to leave, it was evident that there was little future left. On 17 July, the squadron Briefing Room was the setting for a farewell party and, next morning, the squadron paraded before their Commanding Officer, Wg Cdr F.W.L.Wild DFC and was disbanded.

No. 630 Squadron was in existence for only twenty months but it had been a period of continuous action and during that time the unit had earned itself a noble place in RAF history. In a total of 2,453 sorties, including all sixteen raids of the Battle of Berlin, it had dropped 10,347 tons of bombs and laid nearly 800 sea mines in enemy waters. Seventy members won gallantry awards but it had not been without cost, for fifty-nine Lancasters had been lost in action and eleven others had crashed. Within days, their aircraft were flown out and nothing was left of 630 but memories.

East Kirkby's last bombing raid – the 'Eagle's Nest' (Official, via F. Jones)

What lay ahead for 57? 'Tiger Force', a plan to take the weight of at least some of Bomber Command to the Far East was well in hand. Even at that moment, a convoy was being assembled at Panama to transport RAF Regiment and other engineer battalions to construct airfields on islands near Okinawa – still in Japanese hands. No. 57 was among ten squadrons assigned to this 'Long Range Bomber Group', ordered to concentrate on intensive navigation practice.

It came in plenty with the commencement of Operation Dodge. For nearly a year Lancasters were to be used to bring troops home on leave from Italy. Scores of crews were employed on these trips to Bari on the Adriatic coast – a day to go out, a day there and a day to come back. One pilot, Flt Lt John Chatterton DFC,[5] recalls that landing at Bari and seeing the wire mesh runway mat billowing ahead after touch-down was 'interesting'.

Most of their passengers had never flown before and there was little comfort for them – four blankets apiece and a seat on the cold floor as they flew around the Alps via the Carcassonne Gap. But it was their first home leave in years and they didn't grumble. Many a tear must have

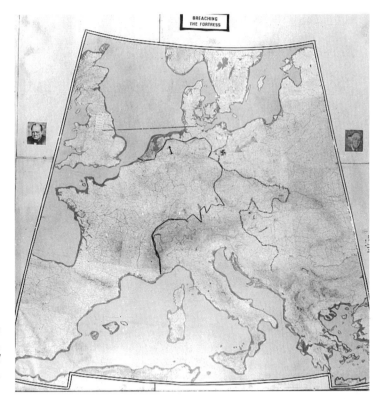

Map in the Intelligence Library on VE-Day, showing meeting of US and Russian troops (Official, via Mrs K. Rowland)

Bob Hamilton (2nd left) and crew, prior to a 'Cook's Tour'. Section Officer Kay Rowland (formerly Seward) was a passenger (Mrs K. Rowland)

Cpls Bache and Bonser with Lancaster LE-U, 'Oh U Beauty' (J.R. Bache)

Flight Engineer Ted Watson about to load 'Window' aboard Lancaster LE-U (E. Watson)

Ground crew 'pressing on'! (J.R. Bache)

Two Aussies try their hand at milking. Bob Hamilton (left) and Tony Hammond, whose sister Joan, the famous contralto, drove an ambulance in the London Blitz (Mrs K. Rowland)

East Kirkby's MT Section (Mrs J. Garraway)

been shed at the first glimpse of the White Cliffs. The Lancaster was a load-carrier second to none but twenty-seven passengers, though carefully arranged around the centre of gravity, was too ambitious and the number was soon reduced to twenty.

Further practice for the work expected over the Pacific came when a series of high-level bombing exercises began. Daily the Lancs could be seen circling and climbing before turning towards the nearby Wainfleet Range. Such a coastal feature was ideal for using the H2S radar but it was soon discovered that at high altitude the open bomb doors distorted the results from the scanner situated in its bulbous housing under the fuselage.

No. 460 Squadron RAAF was another unit assigned to Tiger Force and arrived at East Kirkby from Binbrook on 27 July. Half the depleted crew complement were sent on leave for the first week in August. They had hardly returned when the atomic bombs were dropped and the war in the east came to an abrupt end.

VJ-Day celebrations followed and a week later Tiger Force training was halted. Some may have been looking forward to adventures in the Far East but no one regretted that raids on mainland Japan had now joined the list of 'scrubbed ops'.

Dodge continued throughout the summer and ground crew detachments were eventually based in Italy.

The first Avro Lincoln to enter squadron service, RF385, joined the squadron on 23 August, followed by 386 and 387 a week later. Originally known as the Lancaster Mks IV and V, the Lincoln was some 10 feet longer and had a wingspan 18 feet greater. It carried 50 per cent more fuel, and, at 244 m.p.h., was 50 m.p.h. faster than her predecessor.

Eight selected crews formed the Lincoln Conversion Flight, Sqn Ldrs Michael Beetham[6] and Jones and Flt Lt Chatterton being 'founder pilots'. On their initial flight, Sqn Ldr Beetham and John Chatterton – both of whom had joined No. 630 Squadron to begin a second tour as the war

Sqn Ldr Strachan and Section Officer Grier with their Accounts Section (which includes a couple of frustrated aircrew cadets), East Kirkby, 1945 (A.W. Rowle)

ended – found themselves in a curious position and each was able to endorse the other's logbook as 'Qualified to Type'.

Each pilot on the Flight was to have ten hours of experience on the new type before advancing on to night flying. In parallel with this training, evaluation trials were to be carried out so that maximum hours could be obtained from each aircraft.

The Lincoln was to have been Bomber Command's prime weapon in Tiger Force but, besides being too late, its shortcomings soon became apparent. The planned programme of cross-country flights at up to 20,000 feet was soon beyond reach because of 'teething troubles', especially with the Merlin 85 engines. By the end of September, the three had logged but nineteen hours between them, most of this on air tests and 'circuits and bumps', so that even the crew training was disrupted.

The Lincolns were never used on Dodge but No. 57 Squadron alone flew 560 troops home on leave – and as many back – during September, This, despite problems as Italy's winter rains set in early, covering the metal mesh runways in mud. One Lancaster, PB884, swung on take-off at Bari and was written off but those aboard escaped. No. 460 Squadron joined in the Dodge trips for a while but were soon disbanded prior to going home, 'down under'. Another parade and another party set them on their way on 10 October.

Soon after this the Dodge operation was transferred to Pomigliano, near Naples. Rory O'Brien was a radar fitter on detachment and recalls the scene as Lancasters continued to arrive after dusk: 'Three searchlights met above the airfield and the lights of the circling aircraft with Vesuvius in the background, formed quite a spectacle.'

Lincoln serviceability improved and longer trips were made with two of them as crews

Flg Off Courtney Grebby, Station Fire Officer (J. Monk)

progressed on to four- and three-engine overshoots using 385. It was a unique occasion when the three aircraft flew together alongside a Lanc for a photo-call.

Slowly, the Lancasters were being taken away, one of the first to go being an old favourite, 'C-Charlie', LM517. She first arrived at East Kirkby, brand new, in March 1944, and must have been flown by nearly every 57 crew to serve there since that time. She was a 'workhorse' without compare, flying four ops in seventy hours in one period in July 1944, and taking part in operations on ten consecutive days in August that year. Her journey to Berchtesgaden was her eightieth operation and she retired gracefully. Though many of her stablemates were going to the scrapyard she soldiered on at RAE Farnborough, and escaped demolition until December 1946.

Lincoln 386 continued to suffer engine problems but managed over four hours at 20,000 feet alongside 387 and flew seven hours with 385 a few days later. The exertions grounded her for a month.

The writing on the wall must have been plain for all to see at East Kirkby. 'When will the end come for 57?' They had seen the due ceremony as two other squadrons had disbanded. Despite the obligatory parade on their arrival in the midst of war, when the axe fell, it came as an anti-climax. In mid-November seven three-man crews were 'posted', on paper, to SHQ, tasked with taking the Lancasters away and on 27 November everyone else was simply 'posted out'. The Lincolns went to Scampton and that was that.

No. 57 Squadron had led a varied career, never far from the action, and could claim to have

OLD AIRFIELD

I LIE HERE, STILL, BESIDE THE HILL,
ABANDONED LONG TO NATURE'S WILL,
MY BUILDINGS DOWN, MY PEOPLE GONE,
MY ONLY SOUNDS, THE WILD BIRDS SONG.

BUT MY MIGHTY BIRDS WILL RISE NO MORE,
NO MORE I HEAR THE MERLINS ROAR,
AND NEVER NOW MY BOSOM FEELS,
THE POUNDING OF THEIR GIANT WHEELS.

FROM THE AGELESS HILL THEIR VOICES CAST,
THUNDEROUS ECHOES OF THE PAST,
AND STILL, IN LONELY REVERIE,
THEIR GREAT DARK WINGS SWEEP DOWN TO ME.

LAUGHTER, SORROW, HOPE, AND PAIN,
I SHALL NEVER KNOW THESE THINGS AGAIN,
EMOTIONS THAT I CAME TO KNOW,
OF STRANGE YOUNG MEN SO LONG AGO.

WHO KNOWS, AS EVENING SHADOWS MEET,
ARE THEY WITH ME STILL, A PHANTOM FLEET,
AND DO MY GHOSTS STILL STRIDE, UNSEEN,
ACROSS MY FACE, SO WIDE AND GREEN.

AND IN THE FUTURE, SHOULD STRUCTURES TALL,
BURY ME BEYOND RECALL,
I SHALL STILL REMEMBER THEM,
MY METAL BIRDS, AND LONG-DEAD MEN.

NOW WEEDS GROW HIGH, OBSCURE THE SKY,
O REMEMBER ME, WHEN YOU PASS BY,
FOR BENEATH THIS TANGLED, LEAFY SCREEN,
I WAS YOUR HOME, YOUR FRIEND, "SILKSHEEN".

W. SCOTT,
EX-630 SQUADRON.

This emotive poem, by Walt Scott, former air-gunner with 630 Squadron, is on a plaque on the Squadron's Memorial at East Kirkby. Silksheen was East Kirkby's call-sign (Author)

played its part to the full, having flown well over 5,000 sorties for the loss, in action, of 172 of its various aircraft. Of these, 108 were Lancasters. Additionally, a further 37 of these met with accidents.

The squadron could also claim to have paid its full share of the cost, always suffering the highest loss rates as a percentage of sorties flown. Of Blenheim operations, 17.2 per cent failed to return; the squadron suffered the highest losses among No. 3 Group's Wellington squadrons, and, at 3.34 per cent, the highest in Bomber Command for all aircraft types combined. Nearly two hundred awards for gallantry were made to the men who flew on operations through the Second World War.

NOTES TO CHAPTER 9

1   Of the eight men aboard the No. 207 Squadron Lancaster, ME473, only seven bodies were found. The coroner concerned decided that the one that could not be identified was that of air gunner, Sgt Robert Banks. The remains were buried in a grave marked 'An Unknown Airman'. The eighth body was never found and bomb-aimer Flt Sgt Arthur Henderson was listed as 'Missing, presumed dead', leaving his parents to grieve and wonder for the rest of their days.

In 1995 a licence was issued permitting the excavation of No. 57 Squadron's ND572; during the work, ME473 was disturbed and human remains uncovered. An investigation by the RAF followed and personal effects found made it possible to confirm that the remains were of Sgt Banks.

On 25 October 1996, two ceremonies were held at the RAF Cemetery plot, Cambridge. Sgt Banks was buried with full military honours and wreaths were laid to the memory of Flt Sgt Henderson whose grave will now be marked by a new headstone. Among those present at the ceremonies was Peter Sells (ex-207 Squadron), who had attended the funerals held in 1945.

2   A small party of soldiers of the Pioneer Corps were employed on runway repairs and other maintenance tasks. Enthusiasm led them to lend a helping hand when 'bombing-up' was taking place.

3   To Flt Lt MacBean, Flg Offs Grebby and Gott GM, went awards of the MBE. Cpls Forster and Friswell and LACs Brown and Thaxton received British Empire Medals.

4   Soon after the war, Field Marshal von Rundstedt recorded: 'Air power was the decisive factor in Germany's defeat. Lack of petrol (due to bombing) was the second and the destruction of the railways the third. The other principal factor was the smashing of the home industrial areas by bombing.'

5   John Chatterton had the distinction of having been born 'on the airfield' for, long before the war, his parents had farmed Hagnaby Grange, so lately destroyed in the explosions.

6   Sqn Ldr Michael Beetham DFC was no stranger to East Kirkby, having arrived for the first time by parachute in 1944 when his Lancaster from Syerston crashed in flames beside the airfield. Sir Michael has been no stranger to the RAF since, for he attained the highest rank and became Chief of Air Staff.

CHAPTER 10

The Post-war Years of Change

At Scampton next morning, 28 November, the members of the Lincoln Conversion Flight were in limbo as they observed with interest the way a squadron should really be 'stood down'.

In contrast to 57's cursory dismissal, AOC No. 1 Group (No. 5 Group also being on the point of closure) took the salute as No. 103 Squadron was formally disbanded. Immediately, some of the crews formed up with the Lincoln Flight and a new 57 Squadron marched past the dais.

Never had 'The Body' suffered such change and it might be expected that 'The Spirit' would take time to recover. Under the command of Wg Cdr Renaut, the 'new' squadron was a 'mixed' unit, still having sixteen ex-103 Lancasters on charge.

The crews were soon airborne, five Lincolns taking off for bombing practice and air-sea firing. Next day, six Lancasters were committed to a 'Bullseye' exercise but four were frost-bound and missed the deadline.

The Dodge trips had continued with scarcely a pause, though the value as a navigational exercise paled. Heading across Europe the crews called up specified stations such as Pisa to obtain fixes. John Chatterton, bored with the routine of calling in to recite the numbers from one to ten introduced a variation: 'Twas brillig and the slithy toves did gyre and gimble in the wabe'. Very rarely did it evoke a 'Carrollean response'; usually a pause was followed by the dreary '10, 9, 8 . . .'.

As the Italian weather deteriorated further a hundred or more Lancasters were stranded at Pomigliano, unable to stir off their metal hardstandings because of mud and frost. Some crews were there for weeks, despite 'travelling light' with just a toothbrush and little money. There was, however, an issue of cigarettes and non-smokers such as Chatterton soon discovered a source of wealth. When the crews did get paid, it did not take long to find that the official exchange rate of 400 lire to the pound compared unfavourably with the 1,000 lire a pound note would quickly attract elsewhere. That made cherry brandy a cheap present to bring home.

Several crews spent their Christmas weather-bound, arriving 'home' in January in time to be grounded along with the rest as a blizzard set in, bringing snow and fog which cleared a little by 18 January. As it cleared, there followed a series of 'Eureka' thermometer trials, entailing flights to 20,000 ft. By the end of March, the squadron had become an all-Lincoln unit. As the Lancasters left, eighty aircrew were made redundant and only fifteen crews remained as Wg Cdr K.P. Mackenzie took command.

The move to Lindholme to take advantage of longer runways saw 57 back in Yorkshire after an absence of thirty years. Operation Lashout, a 'War Course', was the only action of note before 11 October, when the squadron was on the move again, back to Waddington.

An air-sea rescue exercise was a let-down. The aircraft involved circled Spurn Head for four hours awaiting a Warwick with an airborne lifeboat but it never turned up. Before Christmas, three Lincolns went out to Malta for bombing practice but bad weather sent them home via St Mawgan, very quickly.

It was a cold welcome for Sqn Ldr R. Sage AFC as he took over command in January 1947. That month saw the worst blizzards that Britain could remember and the RAF was paralysed, as was the rest of the country.

117

View from the port window of John Chatterton's Lancaster at Pomigliano . . . (J. Chatterton)

As the snow cleared in February, the squadron began Operation Seaweed – a series of regular eight-hour flights for the Meteorological Office. Diversions to Lossiemouth became a way of life for the crews thus engaged and the Seaweed work continued during another change of station, to Hemswell, on 28 March.

Engine problems continued to bug the Lincolns, 'blow-back' being a constant worry. On 13 May an aircraft swung on take-off because of this failure, broke her back when the brakes were applied and became a write-off.

The squadron was to carry out its Met. Flights until 1 December 1947, when the commitment was passed to another squadron and 57 became part of the main bomber force once again. Three crews were detailed immediately for Exercise Sunray, which seemed to promise travel overseas, but only two aircraft were serviceable for most of the month and they were able to play no part in it.

It is recorded that petrol supply problems were being experienced at the time, but this appears to have been a 'bulk delivery' difficulty rather than carburation. Despite their problems, or, perhaps in recognition of them, when AOC, No. 1 Group, paid a visit at that time, he complimented the crews for their fine efforts. The squadron was on the move again on 15 December, back to Waddington, though runway resurfacing was incomplete.

The spring of 1948 saw developments in the work plan and on 5 March six aircraft were

. . . and from the starboard (J. Chatterton)

detailed to take part in another Operation Sunray. They fulfilled their task this time, carrying out blind bombing attacks on the island of Filfa, three miles south of Malta, en route for Shallufa, Port Suez. The Sunray series of operations usually lasted a month and this particular exercise was reported as successful. In June a return on the amount of ammunition used on Sunray recorded: .5-inch shells – 13,970; 20-mm shells – 2,440; 25 lb practice bombs – 239. (There was no shortage of 'real' bombs for vast stocks, including 'Cookies', remained in the Canal Zone.)

As Sqn Ldr Ellen MBE took command in the summer the programme of training crews on the Lincolns continued, though there was still no real confidence in reliability. Aircraft being prepared for Operation Dagger, planned for September, were grounded from 28 August to ensure 100 per cent serviceability. Even so, of five involved, three returned on three engines and a week later another suffered a 'blow-back' and became U/S.

The last aircraft movement of consequence that month was apparently trouble-free – a Lincoln was transported to Hyde Park by road to be assembled for exhibition during the Battle of Britain commemorations.

In February 1949, the squadron's number was 'plated' with that of another and became known for some years as '57/104'. That month saw more successful 'Sunray' exercises when six crews and a support party of thirty-four ground crew went out to Shallufa.

'Yoke' was one of the first three Avro Lincoln B2s to enter RAF service (D. Brown)

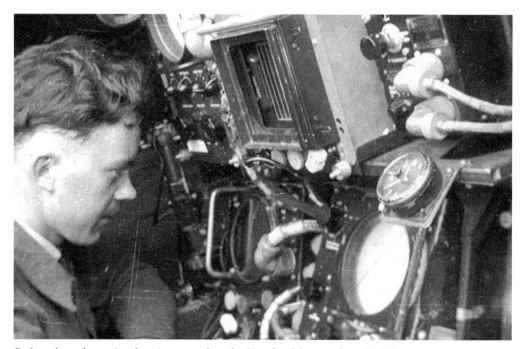

Radar tube and associated equipment on board a Lincoln of the squadron (R. O'Brien)

In June, another major exercise: six aircraft took off in seven minutes to simulate attacks on London, Birmingham, Port Sunlight and the Rolls-Royce engine works at Derby. C-in-C Group paid a surprise visit that night and it was recorded that he was in a very good mood when he left.

At the end of the year, Sqn Ldr Ellen went to Air Staff at Command, his place being taken in due course by Sqn Ldr P.M. Brothers DSO DFC.

In the spring of 1950 Communist rebels were causing trouble in Malaya and it may be that someone recalled the success of the 1920s when aircraft had been used to keep unruly tribes in order. Accordingly, a plan was raised – Operation Firedog – to use a heavy bomber force from the RAF and the RAAF to attack the bandits in their jungle camps.

At short notice, the ground crews were allowed thirteen days in which to paint six aircraft in tropical white, fit long-range tanks and cargo panniers and carry out complete servicing. This was done on time and two more Lincolns from 61 Squadron made up the strength to the required eight.

The aircraft were taken to Lyneham to be disinfected on 10 March. Meanwhile, ground crew, suffering from the 'jabs' against yellow fever, etc., loaded their equipment (and their KDs) aboard Hastings transport aircraft and flew out east, via Castel Benito, Habbaniya and Mauripur. On 20 March, the first four Lincolns to arrive circled Singapore Island in formation and landed at Tengah.

With no hydraulic lifting equipment available bombing-up for the earliest missions was carried out by sheer manual labour and the aircrew joined in the hot, hard graft.

On 4 April 1950, just five years after last dropping bombs in anger, 57 raided an obscure part of the Malay jungle, known only as the Tang Area. Five aircraft dropped sixty 1,000-pounders. The raids continued in this manner for some weeks without untoward incident, though much emphasis was placed on learning jungle survival techniques, including exercises with the Army and the RAF Regiment.

Entertainment was a bit limited; even slaking equatorial thirsts with the infamous Tiger Beer could lose its appeal. Someone was overheard, one morning, suggesting that it might be more effective if they kept the bombs and dropped the beer on the 'commies'! Flt Lt W.C. Sinclair, 'B' Flight Commander, had his own way of defeating boredom. On learning that the Far East Air Force (FEAF) Boxing Championships were imminent, he went to RAF Changi. Thirty-five seconds in the ring was all he needed to return as FEAF Featherweight Champion.

From 17 May, the crews were ordered to make low-level strafing attacks on the rebel camps. It was a very different event in June when the Lincolns joined in a fly-past over Singapore to mark the king's birthday.

Early July saw the squadron return to Waddington, the support staff following them across the world in Hastings and Dakotas. The Lincolns involved in Malaya were then sent to Avro's Woodford works for a short overhaul. Air Bomber Sgt Cook brought honour to the squadron by winning the premium Bombing Trophy with an error of only 84 yards.

In December, a detachment went to Cyprus for exercises. Among the 'exercises' was the delivery of Christmas trees to the hospital at Shallufa and to other units in the Canal Zone. Some of the crews involved actually spent Christmas at Shallufa but most got home for their celebrations.

The New Year of 1951 began with a series of 'Weather Flights' to Gibraltar followed by high-level bombing exercises over Heligoland. These, however, ceased abruptly on 21 March. The Cold War temperature was just about at zero and Britain had plans to become a nuclear power. As the largest bomber in service, the Lincoln lacked an elementary requirement – the ability to escape from the effects of its own weapon. Britain's V-Bombers were still in the development stage and the only available aircraft with an adequate range were Boeing B-29s. Accordingly arrangements were made for a number of these to be acquired on loan from the United States.

And so, on 21 March the unit moved on detachment to the Washington Conversion Flight at Marham to prepare to re-equip once more, this time with the famous 'Superfort', renamed the Washington B1 by the RAF.

With a wingspan of 141 feet 3 in and 99 feet long, this was by far the largest aircraft type that No. 57 Squadron ever flew and the crew complement was enlarged, though the manning level never equalled that of the USAF. The second pilot's seat was occupied, though sometimes by a senior flight engineer. Another engineer, a plotter navigator and radar navigator were carried, plus a signaller. Three or (usually) four air gunners manned the turrets. Many of these were known as 'cadets' and were, in fact, National Servicemen. (They were also known, a little unkindly, as 'Two-year Wonders' or 'Widgets'.)

Certainly speed and range – 351 m.p.h. at 25,000 ft, 1,000 miles with a payload of 11,500 lb, 3,000 miles with 6,000 lb – proved more than adequate. The forepart of the fuselage was pressurized and well heated – each crew position was equipped with a device for heating a tin of soup and even had an ashtray! Compared to the Lincolns they offered sheer luxury.

For both air and ground crews there was much to be learned, for these giant aircraft had very different systems from anything they had met before – and the ground crews soon discovered that no two planes seemed to be alike! Americans arrived to pass on their expertise, particularly civilian 'reps' from companies such as Honeywell and Norden, and of course, from Boeing.

By 1 June the squadron was reported as being established at three aircraft and was at full strength by 25 June. Detachment ceased and, on being transferred from No. 1 Group to No. 3, they returned to Waddington in time for a parade to mark the king's official birthday. By August all crews had flown cross-country and HLB exercises and on 16 August a 'blind attack' was made on the Luqa airfield, Malta.

Engaged in Exercise Circus, Washington WF555 was homeward-bound across France on the night of 29 September when she suffered from an over-speeding propeller on the No. 3 engine. Fragments were thrown off and struck No. 4, putting all the electrical systems thereon out of action. The pilot, Flt Lt Lang, ordered three of the crew to bale out at 17,500 feet over Amiens before he brought off a successful crash-landing at Orly. Though this was accomplished in darkness with neither undercarriage or flaps the remaining crew survived though the aircraft was a write-off.

By February 1952, the squadron was fully equipped with eight Washingtons with the unit-code 'MB'.

Early that year the nation mourned the death of the king. No. 57 Squadron paraded at full strength at Waddington before a detachment was sent to add military presence to the memorial service held in Lincoln Cathedral.

On 1 April, though remaining in No. 3 Group, the squadron moved to Coningsby under Sqn Ldr Holmes and, soon after, was paraded before the AOC Group, an event made much of, civic dignitaries and American guests being present.

Along with the usual work, emphasis was placed on the importance of 'Passive Defence', including protection against chemical and nuclear warfare.

Gerry Beauvoisin served as a Cadet Air Gunner and recalls a moment when a colleague faced a hazard of his own making. After a flight with the flight commander at the controls the gunner became exasperated, noting that the engineer seemed to prefer to supervise post-flight drills, leaving the donkey work of shut-down procedures to the gunners. This gunner pointed to the figure bending down on the tarmac. 'Look at him', he said, 'pretending to put his parachute and

Washington WF554 at Coningsby, 1952 (F.G. Beauvoisin)

No. 57 Squadron taxies out for Exercise Ardent, October 1952 (F.G. Beauvoisin)

The crew of WF554. Captain, Flt Lt Hickmott. Gerry Beauvoisin is 2nd right (F.G. Beauvoisin)

stuff away. Watch this. I'll teach the lazy so-and-so a lesson.' He delivered a boot to the target. The squadron leader straightened up and turned! 'His instant acceptance of the explanation and apology raised our respect for him enormously.'

Other light moments came in July when what was described as a squadron outing to Skegness took place, leaving Coningsby at 10.00 hours and returning at 'midnight or thereabouts'.

There were seventy-eight aircrew (mostly NCOs) on the unit at that time and the month's target of 184 flying hours was reached comfortably. This left time to be filled; there was never a better way than the old fall-back, an escape exercise.

The main event in Exercise Ardent in October 1952 called for 'maximum effort'. No. 57 rose to the occasion, being the only unit to meet the requirement.

April 1953 saw the squadron face enormous changes. They said 'goodbye' to propellers and 'tail-draggers' as the Washingtons were returned to their rightful owners, the US government, to be replaced by English Electric Canberras. Besides the squadron's introduction to the jet age, there was a drastic change in crew make-up as conversion began once more. The Canberras (Mks B2 and T4) carried a crew of three, pilot, navigator/observer and navigator/plotter, reflecting the increased use of radars and other electronic devices. The unit shrank overnight; when Sqn Ldr I.G. Broom DSO DFC began to assemble his command, aircrew strength was just twenty-eight – it had not been so low since the 1930s. These were to man the established eight aircraft, though only five were on strength at first.

Among the earliest assignments was the provision of just one aircraft to take its place among the 640 that formed up for the Queen's Coronation Review at Odiham in July.

Cross-country exercises were rated at high priority. Many were short, three-hour affairs, but by March 1954 experiments in 'Heavy Load Take-off' were on the curriculum. The next month saw the work carried to a fine conclusion with a flight to El Adem, the longest single-stage flight made by the unit. Covering some 1,800 nautical miles at 428 knots the journey took four hours and nine minutes. Further, it was claimed that sufficient fuel remained for another 200 miles, though conceding there had been 'a good wind'!

After a move to Cottesmore in May, there was a notable event on the parade ground when the squadron was honoured in recognition of twenty-five years' active service, with the award of its Standard, bearing the (then) maximum eight Battle Honours. The 104 Squadron 'plate' was removed at that time.

Cross-country flights around the United Kingdom continued, training for tours abroad, along with 'continuation training' for 'GH', a navigational aid. The squadron's establishment was, by now, set at ten aircraft, though only nine were held. Aircrew strength was recorded as: Officers – 35, NCOs – Nil.

The squadron sent six Canberras abroad in November, on a goodwill tour of the Middle East, giving opportunity for tropical experience with the aircraft involved. Displays at Baghdad (Iraq), Amman (Jordan) and Idris (Libya) were enjoyed by all and created a good impression on the thousands of spectators.

Home again, one aircraft made a cross-country flight with one throttle back, 200 knots being held for three hours; the controls were 'comfortable'.

February 1955 saw the squadron on the move again and Honington became their new home base. Training continued along well-established lines, giving extensive practice in long-distance navigation and flying. A flight was sent to Idris/Fayid for Exercise Lone Ranger and two aircraft went to Nairobi. In June, there was Briefing to a target of a decade earlier, though this time the attacks on the railway yards at Osnabrück were only simulated.

VIPs visited Marham in March 1956, and five of 57's crews took their Canberras to join the Vulcans and Hunters in a display laid on for Messrs Bulganin and Kruschev, representatives of the 'rival firm'. The display did not create the hoped-for impression for the weather was so overcast that those taking part could hardly see each other.

The aircraft were grounded for 'mods' in May 1956 and work was carried out to fit them for work in Luqa (Malta) and Idris. A detachment then went out to take part in a Defence of Malta exercise in July. There must have been a little grumbling about the accommodation, for the officers found themselves in other ranks' blocks, while the ORs slept in tents. The set piece of the exercise was a simulated attack on the US Navy's Sixth Fleet. Soon after, several crews went out on detachment to Nicosia, Cyprus, attached to Nos 15 and 44 Squadrons during the Suez Crisis, though they seem to have played little part in this sorry affair.

In November the squadron moved yet again, a return to Coningsby.

A detachment went out to Changi, Singapore, for the first two months of 1957 to carry out photo-reconnaissance work. It was no holiday cruise for the ground crew complement for they found that they had to service their Hastings transport at every stop en route.

By now, under command of Sqn Ldr Arscott, the unit faced a busy summer of NATO and other exercises including detachment at Cappodichino in Italy for June and July. Lone Ranger, a diversionary exercise, and Rosie, Rosie were the last major operations carried out with the Canberras, and in November 1957 the squadron was disbanded once more.

CHAPTER 11

The Victor Era and the Present

Though Britain had its first production atom bombs by the end of 1953, it was not until the completion of the trials in Australia in 1956, and in the Pacific in 1958, that she could claim to have become a nuclear power.

As an interim reinforcement to the nuclear capability while awaiting development and delivery of further weapons and suitable aircraft to carry them, the RAF took on charge sixty Thor Intermediate Range Ballistic Missiles (IRBM) acquired on loan from the United States. Twenty squadrons, mostly bearing the numbers of wartime bomber squadrons, were dispersed around the eastern part of the United Kingdom with three missiles apiece.

Soon the V-Bombers (so-called because of the decision to use names beginning with 'V' for the three aircraft types involved: Valiant, Vulcan and Victor) began to come into service. These were to carry Britain's own new weapons over the Iron Curtain should, God forbid, occasion arise. There could be no doubt that Russia was in a permanently truculent mood for most of those post-war years.

On New Year's Day 1959 No. 57 Squadron re-formed at Honington as part of the V-Force. Under the command of Wg Cdr K.C.M. Giddings OBE DFC AFC, they were to be equipped with Victor B1s, which began to arrive in March.

The Victor was the most capacious of the V-bombers, able to carry a remarkable load of thirty-five 1,000 lb 'iron' bombs. The bomb-bay was tailor-made to fit 'Blue Danube', a 10,000 lb atomic weapon. The maximum speed was put at 640 m.p.h. (Mach 0.92), service ceiling 55,000 feet and range 2,700 miles – a formidable weapon indeed. The captain and second pilot sat side-by-side in ejector seats with the crewmen behind in conventional seats across the aircraft facing to the rear. These three shared a common work table, AEO (air electronics operator) on the port side, nav-radar on the starboard, nav-plotter between.

One of the first flights carried out with the new type looked a little suspect, for the AOC-in-C promptly took one back to the Handley Page works at Radlett, apparently just for the ride. Perhaps he could argue that it was right and proper that he should have some experience of his charges.

As the aircrews, newly qualified at No. 232 Conversion Unit, began to arrive and ground crews were finding their way around these awesome beasts, the squadron diarist looked close to hand for items to note: first, it was recorded that the Orderly Room sergeant had absconded. 'He's done it before; it's a habit. He won't be seen again.' In April, the Station Commander criticized the weeds in the flowerbeds around the squadron offices. 'With respect, sir,' said the Adjutant, 'they are marigolds.' Nature took its course and it cost 'Groupie' a pint. More than a pint was sunk at the first squadron party, held at Thetford, for 'a great deal of beer was consumed. The ham sandwiches, however, would have made good blotting paper.'

Very soon the full complement of eight aircraft was on charge, the last arrival, VH651, being one of the last Mk 1s to be built. As with all the squadron's previous changes of equipment, exercises became a daily routine. One, well off the beaten track, was undertaken by a pair of Victors that flew out to Tehran to take part in the Imperial Iranian Air Force Day in October. They made a remarkable impression, though Lady Luck played her part when a crew door came open during a low-level fly-over.

The three V-bombers: Victor, Vulcan and Valiant (C. Chester-Jones)

The next month a detachment went even further afield. First they went on a training exercise at Butterworth, Malaya, and then were diverted temporarily to represent the RAF in a display at Manila during Philippines Aviation Week.

By 1961 the V-Force had reached peak strength. Seventeen squadrons equipped with 164 bombers occupied thirty-six airfields at various times. A handful of these, Vulcan Mk 2s and Victor B2s later carried the 'Blue Steel' powered stand-off weapon, and some were, for a time, partly answerable to 'Saceur', NATO's Supreme Allied Command, Europe.

Meanwhile, the squadron was on detachment to Singapore once more when trouble reared its head in Indonesia. On 20 July 1962 the squadron was honoured when HRH Princess Marina presented a new Queen's Standard.[1]

As ever, training was a continuous process and with such responsibilities great emphasis was placed on efficiency. Crews were classified according to their prowess, the classification being set at that of the lowest rated member. Competition was fierce between crews, squadrons and other NATO forces. No. 57 Squadron was successful in two contests in 1963. 'The Cock', which since 1957 had been awarded annually to the best medium bomber squadron (medium refers to range) in the Navigational Bombing Systems Competition, came once more into their possession.

The second award won by the squadron that year was the Lawrence Minot Trophy which, since 1957, had been the highest prize in competition for navigation and bombing. The base was engraved with the numbers of many famous squadrons but the trophy had, until now, eluded 57, to whom it had very special meaning.[2]

Various marks of the Handley Page Victor equipped No. 57 Squadron from January 1959 until June 1986. B1, XH616, is shown here in 1959 (C. Chester-Jones)

By now, Bomber Command had developed 'Alert and Readiness Plans'. For the next six years, the crews of 57, along with the other squadrons of the V-Force, followed the unending, unpublicized, Quick Reaction Alert (QRA) routine. For twenty-four hours a day, year in, year out, duty crews were confined to the Station, fully kitted-up and ready to fly at a moment's notice. Much of the time was spent in the crewrooms but the highest state of readiness, determined by the prevailing intelligence situation, required them to occupy the aircraft cabins – for any length of time – waiting, always waiting.

When the 'tele-scramble' signal came engines were started simultaneously and the Victors were airborne within two minutes. Each time, the question: was this one yet another of the no-notice dispersal exercises to send them off to designated airfields, Lone Rangers to the east or Western Rangers to the west, there to await a further 'Scramble'? Or was this the one that had originated at Fylingdales or some other early warning system and might lead to the turning of keys and the pressing of various 'red buttons'?

By 1962, as the Valiants were being withdrawn from bomber service, Nos 90 and 214 Squadrons began to operate them as tankers, supplying the suitably modified Vulcans. By the end of the year the Victors were also being converted to become 'receivers', No. 57 Squadron being the first to be so equipped. They immediately started a series of air-to-air refuelling exercises with the Valiants.

This was most demanding work, for the receiver had to approach the tanker so as to be positioned within 15 in of the centre of the delivery drogue, despite the inevitable buffeting. With a closing speed of 1 to 3 knots proper contact would be made and as the hose wound back a little towards its delivery unit transfer could begin.

The squadron on detachment for bombing practice at Akrotiri, June 1961 (C. Chester-Jones)

Meanwhile, the Soviet bloc had been further developing defensive missiles and extending radar coverage of their 'empire'. A complete change of tactics came about and the V-bombers began to practise low-level operations – they were already equipped with various electronic countermeasures.

Gradually, as if on cue, Britain's nuclear submarine and missile programme came into fruition, heralding the end of the V-Force.[3]

Severe corrosion was found in the Valiants and they were all withdrawn from service that year, a programme to convert the Victors into the tanker role being well under way.

In the middle of 1965 No. 55 Squadron began to operate the first Victor tankers, interim B1A (K2P)s. Late in the year 57, under the command of Wg Cdr H.D. Hall AFC, joined them at Marham and, on 14 February 1966, took delivery of the first K1. This was a '3-point' tanker able to refuel three smaller 'customers' at any one time. As each tanker was taken on charge, a bomber was taken away for conversion.

Externally, the aircraft were much the same. Internally, they were virtually a new aircraft. The bomb-doors were removed and the capacious bomb-bay completely occupied by two tanks, each able to hold 15,300 lb of fuel (over 3,000 gallons in all), and the central Mk 17 HDU (Hose Delivery Unit). Beneath each wing were 'pods' also containing hose units and a probe was fitted to the nose so that the tanker itself could become a receiver. By refuelling in flight, the Victor tanker was permitted to exceed its maximum permitted take-off weight by 10,000 lb!

Further refinements were the fitting of rear-view mirrors to bring the pods into view and a downward-facing periscope so that the HDU and hose could be observed. Swivel seats were fitted for the rear crew members and all communication equipment was changed to the latest available, essential if rendezvous points were to be accurate.

However, the biggest change – and the biggest challenge for the crews – came from the work that was now required. The squadron was fully operational by 1 June as a complete tanker force was assembled at Marham, comprising twenty-four Victor Mk1 and 1As, operated by Nos 55, 57 and 214 Squadrons, along with an Air Refuelling School and Training Flight. (Though the traditional rivalry between squadrons never quite died, loyalties must have been divided, for crew members seemed to 'change sides' on occasion.)

At this time the Russians were increasing their probing flights to test our air defences. Lightnings and Phantoms were also on QRA and were scrambled to intercept any Russian aircraft spotted by radar coming round the North Cape and looking as if they might enter UK airspace. From whichever station the fighters took off, two tanker crews were on constant standby to rendezvous and give support.

Work on development of various techniques continued, and No. 57 Squadron were pioneers in night refuelling – fluorescent tritium cells were fitted around the rim of each drogue to make it visible. In course of time the squadron was to demonstrate its skills on deployment as far afield as Toronto and Hong Kong.

The tankers put on a suitable display for the Anniversary Review at Abingdon in 1968, marking the RAF's fiftieth birthday. That year saw another change in the structure of the Service as Bomber and Fighter Commands combined to form Strike Command.

In January 1969 ten Phantoms left the United Kingdom to fly to Singapore and back, a total of 18,500 miles (29,772 km). Tankers were based at Akrotiri, Masirah and Gan, so that each of the fighters could be refuelled the required thirteen times each, the largest refuelling exercise up to then.

Later that year a Transatlantic Air Race was held to mark the anniversary of Alcock and Brown's first crossing in 1919. Five of 57's tankers took part, acting as filling stations for the Harriers and RN Phantoms that played a successful part in the competition. That same year the squadron won the Sir Alan Cobham Trophy for the most efficient tanker squadron, the first time it had been awarded.

In May 1970 three Phantoms were required to go to Singapore to take part in Exercise Bersatu Padu – Malay for 'unity' – and, to prepare themselves, the crews flew five-lap circuits of Britain, 'topping-up' from the Victors as required on the non-stop, fifteen-hour journeys.

All went well in the practice and in the subsequent flight to Singapore; it took just over fourteen hours, again non-stop, a world record. With similar tanker support, they returned after a month of exercises.

A night-time exercise of note took place early in October when a 57 Victor flying out of Gan refuelled another in darkness.

Someone on the squadron with a sense of history anticipated a rash of celebrations in 1976 as so many squadrons celebrated their Diamond Jubilee. No. 57 decided to 'get in first' and in 1973 held a 57th Birthday Party. Messages from around the world arrived, among them a telegram from Messrs HJ Heinz Ltd, expressing pleasure at knowing that such a fine body was associated with the famous number!

In September 1974 a big NATO exercise, Operation Northern Merger took place, from the Channel to the Norwegian Sea. Phantoms and Lightnings were refuelled by Victors of Nos 57 and 214 Squadrons as they carried out far-ranging fighter interceptions.

Marham presented a damp miserable sight on the morning of 24 March 1975. Sleet swirled about as a Victor took off on yet another exercise, heading roughly north-east. It broke through the cloud into brilliant sunshine and, at about 300 knots, the captain, Flt Lt Keith Handscomb, turned towards the rendezvous point 100 miles east of Newcastle upon Tyne.

Through the lower periscope the navigator could see their 'customers', two Buccaneer fighter-bombers from Honington, drawing near. From the port wing the refuelling hose waited, the cone-shaped drogue waving gently as the first Buccaneer approached. The probe made

No. 57 Squadron's Victor B1A was ceremonially retired to become an exhibit at the Imperial War Museum, Duxford, on 2 June 1975 (Author)

contact and transfer of the fuel began; within two minutes it was complete and the fighter withdrew, 2,000 lb heavier.

The second aircraft approached, the pilot no doubt apprehensive, for this was his first experience of refuelling. In consequence, the first two contacts were to be 'dry', without any transfer. Contact successfully made, he stayed in position for one minute, then drew back, allowing the Victor to turn through 180 degrees. The fighter swept around and followed, aiming once more for the drogue. Suddenly the pilot realized that he was catching up too fast and drew the throttles back as the probe struck the rim of the drogue. The hose snaked around and struck the Victor's fuselage. A split second was all it took for the situation to turn into tragedy. As the Buccaneer drew ever closer, the drogue swung back and hit the canopy. In a desperate attempt to avoid collision, the pilot hauled the control column back, the hose now draped across his fuselage. Dropping down, neither he nor his navigator felt a tremor as the Buccaneer's starboard wing dragged across the port elevator of the larger aircraft.

Losing control, Handscomb ordered his crew to bail out, but as he did so the tail was torn off and the nose dropped. With such 'negative-G' forces there could be no hope of escape for the three crew behind. Almost unconscious from the violent manoeuvre, the pilot managed to get a couple of fingers around the ejector seat handle. Just as he was blown clear, the horrified onlookers aboard the Buccaneers saw the tumbling Victor drop into the cloud, exploding into a ball of flames.

They sent out distress calls before each recovered safely to base. The time was 12.42 p.m.

Air-sea rescue operations were put into action and by one o'clock a Whirlwind helicopter of No. 202 Squadron, Acklington, was on its way, fighting through snow and turbulence beneath the 100 feet cloud base.

Reaching the reported crash site, they found nothing but a spreading oil slick. They began quartering the area and found a large dinghy, half submerged. At great personal risk Master Air Loadmaster Jeff Todd was lowered into the heavy seas to ascertain that it was empty. Next came news that the German freighter *Hoheburg* had found a survivor in a dinghy. The Whirlwind joined in the rescue attempt, and again in great danger, Jeff Todd and two seamen strapped Flt Lt Handscomb into a stretcher. Despite a severely frayed cable, he was winched aboard and flown to hospital, suffering back injuries and exposure.[4]

A few weeks later, thirty years after VE-Day, old comrades of the Second World War gathered together at the site of the former airfield at East Kirkby. It was the first of such reunions, though not the last,[5] and their day was made complete when they were joined by Wg Cdr Alistair Sutherland and a party of serving airmen from the squadron.

The recent loss of their colleagues formed a bond with the older generation present who were glad to share their day of remembrance and memories. They were glad, also, to be guests of the squadron at Marham Families' Day in September, able to see something of the complexities of a Service so changed since their days.

There was a small ceremony at the Imperial War Museum, Duxford, on 2 June 1975, to mark the arrival of Victor Tanker K1A, XH648, formerly a B1A bomber, for permanent exhibition. She was flown in by Flt Lt Handscomb, recovered from injuries and airborne once more. For the occasion he was accompanied by a VIP crew comprising Marham's Station Commander, Gp Capt Parry-Evans, Wg Cdr Sutherland and Sqn Ldr Cunnans. A month later, the first K2 tanker arrived at Marham, but not until January 1977 were the last of the K1s withdrawn from service as No. 214 Squadron disbanded.

The year of the Queen's Jubilee, 1977, was marked by a fly-past down the Mall and over Buckingham Palace. Another spectacular fly-past took place on 29 July, on the occasion of the Queen's Jubilee Review at Finningley. This over-flew a massive static display, watched by the crowds who had gathered that morning to witness a splendid parade as Her Majesty presented a new Colour to RAFUK. It was a unique event, for five other Queen's Colours and all sixty-eight squadron standards were present, the first time all had been gathered together.

In April 1982 Argentina captured the Falkland Islands. The best efforts at peacemaking failed and a task force was assembled to dislodge them. This force left Ascension Island on 16 April, heading south.

Nos 55 and 57 Squadrons arrived on Wideawake, the airfield on Ascension, two days later. Some 4,400 miles (6,500 km) from Britain, it was still the nearest available airfield to the Falklands, a further 3,886 miles on. It was, however, a well-constructed base, with hardstandings for 25–30 aircraft, though its single runway could only be entered or left via the western end.

Despite all that had gone before, it might appear that the tanker force and the Falklands War had been made for each other. It is doubtful if Operation Corporate could have been contemplated without the support of the Victor tanker fleet. In due course, Nos 55 and 57 Squadrons moved to Ascension in toto, leaving No. 232 OCU with just two tankers to complete the ongoing conversion course. Hasty 'mods' were put in hand to enable Vulcans and even Hercules to supply each other. Victors had already done just that to enable one of their number to carry out a photo-recce over South Georgia on 20 April.

Keith Handscomb recalls:

MEMBERS OF NOS. 57 AND 630 SQUADRONS
WHO ERECTED THIS MEMORIAL PAY TRIBUTE
TO THE PEOPLE OF EAST KIRKBY WHO
MADE THEM WELCOME IN BOTH WAR
AND THE PEACE THAT FOLLOWED AND
GENEROUSLY CONTRIBUTED TO THE
MEMORIAL FUND.
THIS MEMORIAL STANDS ON THE
SITE OF THE GUARD ROOM OF THE
AIRFIELD FROM WHICH BOTH SQUADRONS
OPERATED BETWEEN AUGUST 30TH 1943 AND
APRIL 25TH 1945 AND FROM WHICH
OVER 1000 AIR CREW 'WENT MISSING'.

OCTOBER 1979.

Memorial plaque, East Kirkby
(Author)

I was on a ground tour at the time but, as they needed as many pilots as possible, I was rapidly 'got up to speed' again. I went down to Ascension with a Victor on April 29th in 8.25 hours. Between then and September 1st, I flew 66 sorties, totalling 360 hours, the equivalent of what would be a good year's flying by normal standards.

During the campaign the Victors refuelled almost everything that flew. Harriers and Phantoms were topped-up as they were ferried down to Wideawake and, later, to HMS *Hermes* and *Invincible*. Likewise, the range of the Nimrods on their maritime patrols and sub-hunting sorties was extended. Eventually, the load capacity of the Hercules transports taking vital supplies down to Port Stanley was increased by adding fuel after they had become airborne.

However, the most complex operation of all was Black Buck, the bombing of Port Stanley airfield carried out by a Vulcan. On 1 May, as the first of these took off with a load of twenty-one 'iron' bombs, it was followed at one-minute intervals by no fewer than eleven Victors. One of these was a 'spare' and was called into use as another aborted, as did the Vulcan, to be replaced by a back-up aircraft. Flying loosely together, neither type could fly for economy and used fuel at a higher rate than anticipated.

Four Victors passed on their fuel at 840 miles out and returned. Another topped up the Vulcan but stayed longer. A further 300 miles on another transfer took place and two more Victors turned around. A third refuelling was carried out 1,900 miles south of Ascension.

Back at Wideawake the returning Victors, low on fuel, had to all but 'run out of runway' to allow following colleagues room to land.

The Squadron Commander's Mini, airborne for the last time following the disbandment party, 1986 (Author)

A fourth transfer at the 2,700 mile mark had to be carried out at 31,000 feet in a tropical storm of typical violence. Steve Biglands, the pilot of this Victor had a problem; as he replenished tanks from the tanker flown by 57's Bob Tuxford, the probe broke in the extreme turbulence. Consequently, Tuxford had to take his place in order to get the Vulcan to its target. Parting with the necessary fuel for the latter to complete its task left him with insufficient to recover to base. Ditching on the return leg was inevitable unless he could rendezvous with another tanker.

Such an R/V was kept and he was thus rescued from his dilemma. It took yet another top-up to bring the Vulcan home to complete an operation that had lasted almost sixteen hours. Bob Tuxford's efforts had lasted 14 hours 5 minutes and earned him an AFC, his crew receiving Queen's Commendations for Valuable Service in the Air.

Further raids were carried out, aiming at radar installations and troop concentrations. Though the raids were of limited success, no doubt disproportionate to the effort expended, they warned the Argentine government that nowhere was out of reach, causing them to withdraw fighters to defend the homeland. By the end of the short but bloody war, the Victors had flown 3,000 operational hours to complete 530 missions.

Tragedy came unbelievably close to No. 57 Squadron on 15 October 1982. Soon after take-off K2 XL232 suffered a fractured turbine disc which caused damage to the fuel tanks. Recovering to Marham, the entire crew escaped the holocaust that followed the landing as 24,000 lb (9,000 litres) of kerosene burned itself out.

October 1985 saw the squadron providing refuelling support to No. 27 Squadron's Tornados

No. 57 (R) Squadron is tasked with the operational conversion of new crews to fly the Lockheed C-130 Hercules of the Lyneham Transport Wing (Peter R. March)

during the Strategic Air Command Bombing Competition in which the RAF teams won the Le May and Meyer trophies.

Despite careful maintenance, the days of the Victors were numbered; prematurely aged by their 'Corporate' workload they faced early retirement. Their places were to be taken by VC10s, adapted as quickly as possible, though not without problems.

Early in 1986 came the sad news that, once again, 57 Squadron faced disbandment. On her annual visit to 57's home station of Marham that January, Her Majesty the Queen expressed regret at the news and hoped that, one day, the Phoenix might rise again.

This sentiment was echoed by all present at the Disbandment Parade held on 30 June, just weeks after the squadron's 70th birthday. Twenty-six years of service with the Victors ended as the last one made the traditional final fly-past with, perhaps, a traditional misreading of the altimeter?

As the Standard was paraded past the Reviewing Officer, Marshal of the Royal Air Force Sir Michael Beetham GCB CBE DFC AFC (who had, himself, of course, flown with Nos 57 and 630 Squadrons), the young wife of a junior technician lifted her toddler aloft for a better view. Turning to one of the many old 'bomber boys' of the 1940s present she murmured: 'Not a dry eye in the house.' She was not far wrong, for this seemed to be the end of fifty-seven years of operational service, though perhaps a shred of hope remained. Instead of being taken to lie in store or to be a museum piece, the Standard was deposited in the Rotunda at the RAF College, Cranwell.

Meanwhile, Nos 24, 30, 47 and 70 Squadrons were operating Lockheed Hercules from

Hercules aircraft of the Lyneham Transport Wing formate on a Hercules C1K tanker (centre) flown by a No. 57 (R) Squadron crew (Peter R. March)

Lyneham supported by No. 242 Operational Conversion Unit. On 12 October 1992, a decision to revise the status of OCUs to that of reserve squadrons was implemented and 57's 'name-plate' was allocated to 242 OCU. The newly named unit is now No. 57 (R) Squadron, the Hercules Operational Conversion Unit.

Since then No. 57 has carried out its task of preparing crews for work with the thirty or so Hercules C-130s that comprise the Lyneham 'pool'.

Everyone at Lyneham was stunned in March 1993, when Hercules XV193 crashed near Perth with the loss of the nine crew. Soon after this tragedy, crews paraded before the Queen at Marham. Their representative Hercules bore the badges of the five squadrons, all of which had been involved in work for the United Nations High Commission for Refugees (UNHCR) in the former Yugoslavia.

When ex-members of Nos 57 and 630 assembled for a reunion at East Kirkby in the summer, there was surprise and delight to learn that, as well as the eagerly anticipated fly-over by Lancaster PA474, 'City of Lincoln', they were to be visited by another aircraft with four engines and propellers. It was a delight for them to see 'Fifty-seven' back on the old circuit once more after so many years and they appreciated the gesture that proved that the body remained as well as the spirit.

In January 1994, Wing Commander J.S. Wilson assumed command from Wing Commander A. M. Morris.

The Lyneham base is the scene of tremendous activity at times – it has been estimated that

Princess Anne shares the joke with old 'bomber boys'. Left to right: Eric Blanchard, Allen Hudson, Robert Keest, Roy Jones (J. Holsgrove)

the C-130s there are subject to about twice the annual usage of those of the USAF. For example, by January 1995, their aircraft had airlifted over 22,000 tons of relief supplies to the desperate people of Somalia. In June that year Operation Cheshire involved the transport of troops and equipment to Bosnia. Eighty-five crews were used and their day began at 03.00 hours, each aircraft making two round trips of ten hours duration to Split.

Though one of the smallest flying units in a rapidly diminishing Service, the Phoenix continues a tradition founded over eighty years ago. Perhaps this was recognized on 11 September 1995, a special day for No. 57 Squadron, when HRH the Princess Royal presented a new Standard.

NOTES TO CHAPTER 11

1   The Battle Honours held are as follows:

Western Front 1916–18*	Amiens*
France & Low Countries 1939–40*	Norway 1940*
Channel & North Sea 1940*	Ruhr 1941–3*
Berlin 1941–3*	Fortress Europe 1941–4
France & Germany 1944–5*	Walcheren 1944 South Atlantic 1982

The honours marked thus * are emblazoned on the standard.

2   In the form of an eagle, standing some 3 feet high on its ebony plinth, the Laurence Minot Trophy had been awarded originally for the best performance by a pilot and bomb-aimer in the Wessex Area of ADGB. It was fitting that, at last, this magnificent piece had come into the custody of No. 57 Squadron, having been donated anonymously to the RAF in 1926, dedicated 'To the memory of Lieutenant Laurence Minot MC, killed in combat over Meubbeke, Flanders, 27-7-17.' (Lieutenant Minot, who had played such a noble part in the squadron's 'day of great events', 27 July 1917, was in fact killed on 28 July.)

3   The QRA requirement of the V-Bombers was no longer needed when the nuclear submarines came into service in June 1969. In a written Parliamentary answer, the Minister of Defence, Mr Denis Healey, paid but a small compliment 'on the way in which the officers and men concerned at all levels of the Royal Air Force have discharged their arduous responsibilities for the last twelve years'.

4   As a result of his gallantry, MALM Todd was awarded a second Queen's Commendation for Valuable Service in the Air, the first airman to be so honoured.

5   The event proved so successful that many such have been held since and a memorial was erected at East Kirkby in 1979. There have also been remarkable developments there in later years.

Commanding Officers

57 SQUADRON

Maj Sir L.A. Pattinson MC	12 June 1916
Maj C.A.A. Hiatt MC	4 November 1917
Maj G.C. Bailey	11 September 1918
Sqn Ldr H.G. Bowen MBE	20 October 1931
Sqn Ldr F.W. Trott OBE MC	19 January 1933
Sqn Ldr F.W. Walker	26 March 1934
Sqn Ldr F.H.E. Reeve	15 July 1935
Sqn Ldr W.L. Payne	14 December 1936
Wg Cdr H.M.A. Day AM	31st August 1939
Wg Cdr A.H. Garland	14 October 1939
Wg Cdr R.H. Haworth Booth	15 December 1939
Wg Cdr A.H. Garland	7 February 1940
Wg Cdr S.S. Bartram	24 February 1941
Wg Cdr J.M. Southwell	8 May 1941
Wg Cdr M.V. Peters-Smith DFC	16 March 1942
Wg Cdr E.J. Laine DFC	30 July 1942
Wg Cdr F.C. Hopcroft DFC	23 September 1942
Wg Cdr W.R. Haskell DFC	28 July 1943
Wg Cdr H.W.H. Fisher DFC	19 August 1943
Wg Cdr H.Y. Humphreys DFC	15 April 1944
Wg Cdr J.N. Tomes	8 January 1945
Wg Cdr M.W. Renault	23 November 1945
Wg Cdr K.P. Mackenzie	6 March 1946
Sqn Ldr R.J. Sage AFC	20 June 1947
Sqn Ldr R.A.G. Ellen MBE	21 July 1948
Sqn Ldr P.M. Brothers DSO DFC	1 February 1950
Sqn Ldr L.G. Holmes DFC AFC	29 October 1951
Sqn Ldr I.G. Broom DSO DFC	15 May 1953
Sqn Ldr J.F. Rothwell	3 November 1954
Sqn Ldr R.H. Arscott	26 August 1957
Wg Cdr K.C. Giddings OBE DFC AFC	3 January 1959
Wg Cdr D.G. Bailey	19 May 1960
Wg Cdr J.R. Mason	22 June 1962
Wg Cdr R.A.A. Smith DFC	24 July 1964
Wg Cdr H.D. Hall AFC	9 January 1966
Wg Cdr G.C.D. Goodyer MVO	29 May 1968
Wg Cdr H.T.C. Farmer	15 April 1970
Wg Cdr T.J. Newman	2 June 1972
Wg Cdr M.A. Sutherland MBE	26 May 1974

Wg Cdr J.S.B. Price	7 June 1976
Wg Cdr R.C. Betts	1 August 1977
Wg Cdr R.G. Curry	1 February 1980
Wg Cdr A.M. Bowman MBE	11 December 1981
Wg Cdr D. Hayward OBE	4 January 1984
Wg Cdr A.M. Morris	1 June 1992
Wg Cdr J.S. Wilson	21 January 1994
Wg Cdr R.D. Jenkins	13 December 1996

630 SQUADRON

Wg Cdr M. Crocker DFC	15 November 1943
Wg Cdr J.D. Rollinson DFC	12 December 1943
Wg Cdr W. Deas DFC	1 February 1944
Wg Cdr L.M. Blome-Jones DFC	12 July 1944
Wg Cdr J.E. Grindon DFC	September 1944
Wg Cdr F.W.L. Wild DFC	April 1945

My Most Thrilling Flight

A.C.S. IRWIN (LATE RFC)

He recalled that day in 1917, July 27th. There had been a spell of bad weather and little flying. In consequence, the nightly tender to St Omer was usually packed with pilots and observers on pleasure bent. He remembered 'two very fine houses known as No. 1 and No. 4. What these numbers meant and what happened to 2 and 3 I do not know'. [Quite, but what about this flight? – Ed.]

By three o'clock it looked as if the rain would continue till dusk, 'so I decided to change into my pinkest riding breeches and smartest riding boots preparatory to a visit to . . .' [No! No! Get on with the flying. – Ed.]

It was extraordinary what a good impression pink riding breeches and riding boots made with . . . [Deleted by Editor. Now let us get on with the flight. Ed.]

The Editor's prompting succeeded and Captain Irwin told his story of the afternoon's action when the weather cleared.

They had a clear flight to the target and the bombs were dropped with mixed success.

Coming home was very different. Without the bombs, they became a flight of fighters 'capable of catching – or running away from – everything except the latest German scouts'. Irwin dived on a lone 'hostile' and it was shot down out of control.

Suddenly the sky was full of the enemy. 'My superiority complex vanished in a flash . . . with my observer there I couldn't just run for it. How often had we discussed what we would do when we met the great Circus – over numerous glasses of port in front of a nice warm fire, with a gramophone playing somewhere in the corner? It had all seemed so easy.'

Soon he was mixed up in a dog-fight. 'As soon as you got your sights on a machine there would be a rattle from behind and bits would fly off.' He tried to avoid attacks – one explosive bullet into the tank would put an end to everything. 'No more supper parties or theatres.'

They were outnumbered by nearly six to one and usually surrounded by three or four of the enemy – 'black and white checks, stripes, red and white diamonds, serpents and spots, in endless colours and designs'.

From below zoomed a red Albatros. Irwin's observer, Leete, shot his 'V' strut away and down he went. Away went Irwin's right-hand mirror and a piece of the centre section strut. 'Another burst from behind, a sharp pain in my foot and a long rent in my leather coat.' He began to spin, came out facing the sun and escaped.

Safely on the ground, his foot began to hurt but, 'thanks to the beautiful tight-fitting riding boots, now completely ruined, not much blood was lost. That night Minot and Leete came to see me in the hospital at St Omer with Major Pattinson.

'Minot had lost his observer, so he and Leete decided to go into partnership, and what a combination it promised to be.

'But, no! They said they would come and see me again the next night, but they did not come. They never came back.'

Bibliography

1. UNPUBLISHED PRIMARY SOURCES

Documents in the Public Record Office, Kew, Surrey, including various pieces indexed AIR 1, 24, 25 and 27.
Photo Archive in the Imperial War Museum, Lambeth Road, London.
Air Historical Branch, MOD, Great Scotland Yard, London.
Archives in the Royal Air Force Museum, Hendon.
Miscellaneous papers belonging to the author.

2. PUBLISHED SECONDARY SOURCES

Baring, M., *Royal Flying Corps HQ 1914–18*, Blackwood, 1968.
Copeman, G.D., *Silksheen: The History of East Kirkby Airfield*, Leicester, Midland Counties Publications, 1989.
Courtney, F., *Flight Path*, Kimber, 1973.
Falconer, J., *RAF Bomber Airfields of World War 2*, Shepperton, Ian Allan, 1992.
Gale, C., *Royal Air Force, 1918*.
Garbett, M. and Goulding, B., *Lancaster at War 2*, Shepperton, Ian Allan, 1979.
Gibbons, F., *The Red Knight of Germany*.
Harris, A.T., *Bomber Offensive*, Collins, 1947.
Holmes, H., *Avro Lancaster: The Complete Production and Operational Record*, Shrewsbury, Airlife Publishing, 1996.
Jackson, R., *Before the Storm: The Story of Bomber Command 1939–42*, Arthur Barker, 1972.
Johnson, J.E., *Full Circle*, Chatto & Windus, 1964.
Jones, H. and Raleigh, W., *The War in the Air*, 2 vols, HMSO, 1969.
Lawrence, W.J., *No. 5 Bomber Group*, Faber, 1951.
Lee, A.G., *No Parachute*, Jarrold, 1968.
Lewis, C., *Sagittarius Rising*, P. Davies, 1966.
Macmillan, N., *Into the Blue*, Jarrold, 1969.
Middlebrook, M., *The Nuremburg Raid*, Allen Lane, 1973; revised edn Penguin, 1980.
Moyes, P.J.R., *Bomber Squadrons of the RAF and their Aircraft*, Macdonald & Jane, 1964.
Purnell, *Fighters of World War One*, Phoebus Publishing, 1976.
—, *Bombers 1914–18*,
Reynolds, Q., *They Fought for the Sky*, Pan Books, 1974.
Robertson, B., *Lancaster – The Story of a Famous Bomber*, Hemel Hempstead, Harleyford Publications, 1964.
Smith, S., *'Wings' Day*.
Verrier, A., *Grand Strategy: The Bomber Offensive*, Batsford, 1968.

Whitehouse, A., *The Fledgling*.
Winfield, R., *The Sky Belongs to Them*, William Kimber, 1976.

3. MAGAZINES AND NEWSPAPERS

Air Mail
Aeroplane Monthly
Flight
FlyPast
News Chronicle
Popular Flying
Royal Air Force News
Sunday Express
The Aeroplane

Index